The International Series in

ELEMENTARY EDUCATION

Consulting Editor

JOHN M. KEAN
University of Wisconsin

The Critical Years:
Early Childhood Education at the Crossroads

The Critical Years: Early Childhood Education at the Crossroads

EMMY LOUISE WIDMER

Florida Atlantic University

INTERNATIONAL TEXTBOOK COMPANY

An Intext Publisher

Scranton, Pennsylvania 18515

Acknowledgment for photographs is gratefully made to
Palm Beach County

ISBN 7002-2277-4

COPYRIGHT © 1970
BY INTERNATIONAL TEXTBOOK COMPANY

To the Memory of My Mother

Foreword

These are confusing times for those young people who are just coming into the teaching profession. It is for old-timers, too. There are those who say they know exactly what to teach young children and the earlier, the faster, the louder they do it the better. Far in the other direction are those who contend that there should be little or no adult influence on the timing, the methods, or the content of learning. Somewhere in the middle are those who follow a reasonable plan designed on the years of child study, knowledge of the basic needs of children, understanding of growth processes, recognition of the ways young children learn, awareness of the boomeranging pressures of the day, and the consequent necessity to protect the mental health, not only of the children, but of their parents as well.

Danger signs are all around us. There is the adolescent still in high school but "turned off"—not interested in learning. Others escape though various drugs. An alarming number, according to the Commission on Violence, are turning to crime. Younger children are involved in senseless violence. Very young children who are naturally active are given tranquilizers by parents who want quiet and conformity. We may well ask if they need tranquilizers at five what will they be taking at 15?

Early childhood is the time vital attitudes and commitments are etched in. Concern for others, trust, acceptance of valid authority, belief in self do or do not develop depending on the experiences and relationships life offers. Our future is indeed embedded in our children.

This book appears at a fortuitous time. More and more states are mandating Kindergartens. Many teachers who formerly taught older children and many young people emerging from college must man these centers for young children. They need help in attuning themselves to the ways of young children and in understanding and designing good programs for them. This book offers clarification of values and also, particularly in Chapters 4 and 5, practical program content.

Those involved in Head Start and in Child Care Centers will benefit from this book as well. For by whatever name a center for young children may be called the same needs and imperatives exist. They claim our best efforts if we are to develop healthy children for a healthy society.

Alice V. Keliher

Peterborough
New Hampshire

Preface

As the Indian observed upon his first visit to a lighthouse, "Ugh. Bell clang, horn blow, but fog roll in all the same." *The Critical Years: Early Childhood Education at the Crossroads* came into being in answer to a pressing need of the times. We no longer need to be made aware of the children in our midst, as in times past. However, there are disturbing signs that we are viewing childhood as an obstacle on the long and often rough road toward maturity; an uncomfortable period which merely requires pressure and specialized techniques to shorten, if not entirely eliminate. The fog rolls in and threatens to engulf our young in a morass of ill-conceived, hothouse environments with little regard for this imaginative, curiosity-ridden, charming period itself: early childhood. If telescoping growth from crib to adulthood were possible in an age of scientific marvels, what would we actually have accomplished and at what cost in terms of total adjustment and full, rich living?

Thoughtful goals for children become a crucial issue in the midst of this challenging, turmoil-ridden age in which change is the only constant. The pressing need in this last third of our twentieth century is to develop insight and sensitivity to children as children, within the framework of the fantastically rapid scientific and technological progress that dwarfs any minute advances we may have achieved in human interpersonal relationships.

The impressionable early years constitute the base from which attitudes, habits, values and later abstract, formal learnings grow. If this foundation is firmly built upon comprehensive understandings of our young and these understandings are reflected in the programs, methods, curricular materials, equipment, and organizational patterns we devise, it is a sound base from which to carry on the business of living and learning.

We can be more effective guides if we comprehend the what, the how, and the why of early childhood programs in terms of developmental expectancies. In keeping with this theme, the overall goal of this text is to illuminate and to encourage acumen of children and program so that optimal guidance and a stimulating, satisfying environment will become a reality for all young children during their critical early years.

The important position which this early segment of the educational continuum occupies is reflected in chapters devoted to a brief history of early childhood from a modern-theories approach; issues and controversies of concern to thoughtful educators and parents in the world of today; similarities between this early childhood portion and the elementary grades; the differences that necessarily exist, what they are, and the reasons for their being.

Since optimal program is based upon understanding of the child population for which it is designed, the text also includes sections on this developmental period; concept formation and its role in children's learning and thinking; an analysis of the cognitive levels of development in the early years; the role of nutrition; consideration of the special problems inherent in dealing with children of physical and emotional poverty, as well as the curriculum itself and the program design for these early years.

This then is the rationale—the what, the how, and the why of *The Critical Years*.

Grateful acknowledgment and special appreciation is expressed to my parents, who helped this book to become a reality in inestimable ways; my son and the groups of youngsters with whom I have lived and worked, whose avid curiosities and interests keep me ever mindful that growth is a force to be reckoned with; and to the dedicated teachers, supervisors, administrative personnel, and parents it is my pleasure to have known, since it is they and their kind who are the front-line action in any worthwhile educational endeavor.

E. L. W.

Boca Raton, Florida
February, 1970

Contents

      What Is It?
      Insights Gained
      Why Play?
      Summary

Suggested Readings 38

PART II   CONCERNS FOR THE THOUGHTFUL ... 47

   Chapter 3   Childhood: Past and Present 49

      Roots of Early Childhood 49
         A Brief History of the Preschool
         Early Education in Europe
         The Kindergarten in the United States
         Montessori and Early Childhood

      Current Concerns 58
         The Tigers in Our Midst
         Help Offered
         The Time Is Now
         Where We Stand

   Chapter 4   Why Kindergarten? 67

      Achievements 68

      The Kindergarten and Growth 68
         What Else Does Kindergarten Do?

      Role of the Elementary School 71
         The Kindergarten and the Elementary School

      Differences 73
         Focus

   Chapter 5   The Self-Concept 75

      Important Psychological Discovery 75
         Development of the Self
         Keeping in Touch
         A Look at the Child
         Opportunities for Expression
         Summary

Part I

The Formative Years:
Before Six

Chapter 1

How They Grow

INTRODUCTION

Utopia Discovered

Early childhood—that period between the fumblings of diapered toddlerhood and the middle years of childhood with their surge toward full-fledged entrance into the subculture of adolescence—has assumed new national prominence. It has become a repository for national hopes built around development of an articulate, integrated, well-adjusted, intelligent citizenry capable of coping with anything the world of the nebulous future has in store. It is expected to meet the challenge of preparing millions of young children from poor and underprivileged home environments to break the poverty cycle of lack of training, unemployment, ignorance, and fear. A nation is turning to its young in the formative, impressionable, tender years of early childhood as the answer to its dilemmas and festering ills.

This is a tall order for any group, one replete with glorious promise as well as inherent pitfalls. Early childhood has finally come into its own. This new awareness of the importance of early childhood, as well as childhood in general, is evident in the mass media of communication. Tons of paper pulp are devoted every year to articles and syndicated columns about children, books about and for children, magazines about and for children. Many products on grocery, cosmetic, toy, and drug counters throughout the land are frankly devoted to the juvenile trade, or the parents of juveniles. The absorption displayed by parents and interested citizens in the schools children attend is greater than ever before, and shows signs of increasing. The interest displayed in children not only by parents and educators, but also by psychiatrists, anthropologists, psychologists, pediatricians, sociologists, and scientists is phenomenal. Madison Avenue advertising agencies, realizing that the potency of the nation's youth extends to the family's purse strings, have capitalized on the opportunity.

This new awareness of the importance of childhood is evidenced in the labeling of our century as "The Century of the Child."

Paradox or Promise?

Does it deserve its budding reputation which seems to promise all things to all people? What is so special about this developmental period that it seems to guarantee so much to so many?

Stone and Church pinpointed the developmental possibilities of the early childhood youngster when they claimed that he can perform prodigies of development if given a rich and stimulating environment.[1] Hunt highlighted this period and its rich promise when he noted his interest and excitement in encountering people "who are generally considered sensible, planning to utilize preschool experiences as an antidote for what we are now calling cultural deprivation and social disadvantage."[2]

Scott, in summarizing research information on critical developmental stages, indicated that it is during the time of initial socialization that the period of greatest plasticity occurs.[3] This plasticity, this moldable quality, this high receptivity of early childhood youngsters was noted by astute observers centuries ago.

> Everyone knows that whatever disposition the branches of an old tree obtain they must necessarily have been so formed from its first growth, for they cannot be otherwise. . . . Man therefore in the very first formation of body and soul should be moulded so as to be such as he ought to be throughout his whole life.[4]

In his influential book, *The School of Infancy*, published in 1628, John Amos Comenius was not content with merely illuminating the old adage, "As the twig is bent so grows the tree." Instead, he presented methods by which parents and educators might guide the child during the early years. *The School of Infancy*, according to Comenius, was the first and most important of the four schools to which the child was exposed, since it encompassed the first six years of the child's life. "At this early age the unfolding mind resembled wax which will take any impression when it is soft."[5]

Today, three centuries later, authorities agree that the foundation for the child's future social, emotional, physical, and mental growth is built during this formative, plastic period; for it is during infancy and early childhood that the basic attitudes and habits of the child are formed.

Satisfying experiences during these early years are basic to the child's present growth and development as well as later achievements. Even though there is no consensus in regard to the kinds of encounters the child should have with his environment, there is agreement on the following: a child's first five years are crucial ones because of the rapid development which takes place during this time. Influential educational groups, such as the Educational Policies Commission and the National Society for the Study of Education as well as workers in a variety of disciplines, have attested to the importance of this period by giving special consideration to it. A study of the research reveals that these years before six are recognized as critical ones for educational growth as well. It is important what we do with these years.

DEVELOPMENTAL EXPECTANCIES

A Mixed Blessing?

This is all to the good. Children are bound to benefit from this increased awareness. The blessing can be a mixed one, however. If this increased awareness of the importance of childhood is coupled with a lack of understanding of what makes our children tick, it is a mixed blessing. If it is coupled with pressure on children to succeed on an adult level before they are prepared or ready, again it is a mixed blessing.

However optimistic our generation may be in regarding the promise of this early childhood period, warnings are in order. Hechinger's statement is a succinct summary:

> The preschool experiment sounds so logical and so promising that it has begun to appear to some of those embroiled in political and educational battle as a magic escape hatch. . . . There are danger signs that the preschool venture will, by some naïve or opportunistic persons, be treated as patent medicine—oversold as a sure cure, followed by the fatal letdown of disappointment.[6]

The erroneous concept that the preschool is a period of marking time is slowly disappearing. However, a new danger has appeared: the pressure to succeed and to learn difficult subject matter earlier than ever before. This pressure has permeated even the kindergarten and nursery school. If parents and teachers do not know the reasons for the experiences children have in the good early childhood school, they cannot be effective allies and partners in the education of the young child. Nor can they withstand the insidious pressures being brought to bear, some of which, research suggests, may actually be unsound and quite possibly harmful.

What He Is Like

This early childhood period is a particularly charming one, in spite of the bumps, bruises, and annoyances that are a part of any stage or phase of a child's development. Children at this level seem to express themselves more freely than at any other period of development —a characteristic that lends itself well to study. These years of maximum spontaneity, of openness, give us striking insights into these children's own world.[7] Understanding this child is the first step in helping him to grow and develop best. Kyle emphasized this when he stated that people with a knowledge of child growth and development have accruing to them more power than those lacking such knowledge.[8] This knowledge of child growth and development, he continued, can change our understanding, feelings, and behavior toward children and youth, as well as the ways we organize for instruction and the ways in which we work together.[9]

We have a good idea of what to expect in developmental terms. All youngsters travel the growth road. Some may travel it at a speed of ninety miles an hour. Some may travel at the speed of the tortoise in the delightful tale of the Tortoise and the Hare. Some vary their speed. All youngsters will have stops along the way, detours in the road when progress is halted. There will be pauses when growth seems to be at a general standstill. It helps to remember, in the midst of false starts, stops, fluctuations in speed, and many side trips which harry and worry those who live and work with them, that children do move in the general direction of growth. Unless, of course, they are in an environment which is depriving them of essential growth elements such as love, affection, understanding, nutritious food, care for their physical needs, and opportunity for thinking and doing. Such children are the unfortunates, the product of physical and spiritual poverty.

The Whole Child

An important concept is emerging more strongly in the thinking of individuals from various disciplines who are concerned about children as living bodies and not merely as efficient machines. Dr. Edward

Zigler, Director of the Yale University Child Development Center, stated it well when he countered that there is a lot more to life than the formal computer between our ears. We must approach the child as a dynamic, ongoing system, not a limited input-output retrieval system.[10]

Just as concerned medical practitioners are expressing misgivings over the highly specialized, segmented approach to the patient which has emerged during these years of rapid scientific progress; so, too, are thoughtful educators on guard against the loss of the whole-child concept in our zeal for increased understanding about the materials, methods, organizational patterns, and equipment for learning. We are dealing with a complex, living child who cannot safely be compartmentalized into affective, cognitive, motor, and similar domains.

Which brings to mind Deborah of the eager eyes and nimble feet in a nursery school group of three-year-olds one cool autumn day. The youngsters were getting ready to go to their outdoor playground and a few needed help with intractable zippers and buttons. "Close your eyes," said Debbie as the author approached to help her. This can be a foolhardy compliance for the unwary, since early childhood youngsters are notorious for their delight in handling squirming insects and in sharing this delight with the unsuspecting. However, since the request did not include "hold out your hand," it seemed safe to comply. "Open them now," she commanded. Deborah had zipped up her own jacket. "That's wonderful, Debbie!"

She beamed and said, by way of explanation, "I growed bigger!"

The child is a whole. He develops as a whole. He must be considered not only in relation to his mental development, but in relation to his physical, social and emotional development as well. The whole-child concept is supported by investigations which indicate that the child cannot be understood properly when one area is studied without reference to the other areas of his development. His two legs carry not merely a curious mind to school, but also a body which has certain needs pertaining to its level of development. This body can color the learnings that do or do not go on. The child's emotions color his learning; his need for affection and recognition affect his learning, also. A child cannot learn well if he feels sick, if he has not had enough sleep or nourishing food, if he is unhappy, worried, insecure, or unloved.

His head works best when he is happy, secure, well nourished, rested, and loved.

*Total development, including physical and health
needs, is promoted.*

When a child goes to school he carries his head, his body, and his heart with him. All of these need attention.

This whole-child concept leads the thoughtful observer to an important corollary: A child is his own model. As concerned mediators and guides, we must search for areas of strength and weakness within the child himself. We do not compare him with the child down the block who adds like a machine or who talks like a tape recorder. We do not compare him with the boy across town who read the *New York Times* at age two. We compare him with himself, as he was before and as he is now.

This regard for the whole child represents progress.

Patterns of Growth

Each child has a pattern of growth. He shares this general pattern of growth with other youngsters. Through observation of many children it has become possible to establish these patterns or trends. Child growth follows a sequence, and it is a continuous process. Every child passes through these stages or trends of development, although not necessarily at the same chronological age, and each of these stages or trends of development has certain characteristics that help to set it apart, give it a certain flavor. Growth patterns change with maturity and experience, and they can be modified by forces both within and without the body.

There is a warning to be repeated, however. Growth patterns are not uniform for every child, nor are they uniform within a child. Growth is not even in tempo, which is the origin of that meaningful term "the jagged growth profile." Even though physically he may be a giant for his age, his growth in other areas may not match his obvious height and/or weight advance.

Each child is unique. Imhoff stated it well:

> In the use of . . . charts and all comparable data and materials showing the *average* or typical characteristics of a chronological age, there must be recognition of the fact that no real *average child* exists; that such a portrayal of average is a listing of the characteristics most commonly found in children of a particular age through cross-sectional studies (status studies) of many children. Each child, however, according to his individual developmental pattern differs from the *average* or *norm* in varying degrees for each characteristic. Too, as a whole individual, the child's *total* personality is unique to himself; he will differ from all other children even though he may be one within the *average* group.[11]

No child is a carbon copy of anyone else on earth. Herein lies a prize challenge to the researcher in a laboratory context as well as to the teacher of children in an educational setting.

This brings to mind the charming and meaningful poem by John Kendrick Bangs about the elf:

> I met a little elfman once,
> Down where the lilies blow.
> I asked him why he was so small
> And why he did not grow.
>
> He slightly frowned, and with his eyes
> He looked me through and through.
> "I'm quite as big for me," he said,
> "As you are big for you."[12]

Growth is a partnership approach, with genotype and phenotype both in force. Piaget writes about the twin operations of assimilation and accommodation, by which the child reacts to environmental stimuli and, in the doing, is altered thereby as he tries to make sense out of and cope with his environment. Basic to Piaget's developmental viewpoint is the notion that a "proper discrepancy" must exist between what a child already knows and can do, and the new demands made upon him in order for optimal growth to occur. If the discrepancies are too great to be accommodated, then there is danger of frustration and withdrawal. Hunt notes that experience and maturation are continually changing the child's "schemata." There must then be continual concern with the appropriateness of the match between child and environment when we attempt to maximize the richness of an environment in order to produce maximum growth.[13]

Children grow, build their concepts, skills and attitudes through interaction with their environment. The child's growth and learning is given direction and depth through the quality of the environment, and the meaning of the expérience to him.[14]

Axline poignantly described a five-year-old boy's search for self:

> As this child came forth to meet the abrupt forces of life, there grew within him a new awareness of selfhood, and a breathless discovery that he had within himself a stature and wisdom that expanded and contracted even as do the shadows that are influenced by the sun and clouds.[15]

Someone else's schedule may be an artificial graft with no regenerating properties for this child. Children have the right to become themselves, a right to their individuality. They must find their own

best way to their versions of the good life, and we must have the
courage to help them find it.

It takes courage to let a child become himself. Our training is
generally in terms of what we think he ought to become. This kind of
forced "becoming" turns out to be foreign territory for him with
no connection to the real person he is. This training, by its very nature,
will likely set him on the road which leads to various forms of mal-
adjustive behavior, rebellion, dissatisfaction and unhappiness.

Characteristics Seen as Resources

Certain dominant themes seem to recur throughout the early
childhood period from two to six years. These themes include receptivity, "seeking tendencies," vitality, freedom and creativity, spontaneity, imagination, impulsiveness, individualism, curiosity, ego-
centricity, predominant object-and-action orientation, play behavior
and restlessness. A Bobroff signified:

> The pattern of child development, in an over-simplified but
> perhaps useful statement is one of dialectic upward vacillation from
> individualism through conformity and finally to a combination
> of social-yet-singular being.[16]

Research studies have revealed "seeking tendencies" and a high
level of receptivity in this age group as compared with older children.[17]
This early childhood youngster exhibits freedom and creativity, "un-
hampered by tradition or repeated inhibiting experiences, which ren-
ders him especially ready to see, hear, taste, and feel as many new
things as can be provided."[18] And, as Hunt has wisely underscored,
the greater the variety of situations to which the child must accommo-
date his behavioral structures, the more mobile and differentiated they
become.[19] Stated another way, the more a child sees and hears new
things, the more he is interested in seeing and hearing things.[20] It is
quite possible to create beneficial cycles.

A beneficial cycle is in effect in the case of advantaged children
from environments which include vital ingredients of emotional, physical, and intellectual nurturance. The healthy, trusting, curious, active, happy child moves confidently about in his life space. He is perhaps the world's original do-it-yourselfer. Many of his characteristics
during these early years can be considered built-in resources for learning about his environment. If we utilize these natural resources in our
programs for young children, there is less danger of jumping on the
wrong educational bandwagons which lead to the rear.

This early childhood youngster's awesome physical activity and energy is an illustration of a characteristic which is instrumental in affording him understandings. Through the firsthand exploration, manipulation, and experimentation so integral a part of an active child's day, much learning proceeds. It seems there is always more energy, more seeking, more curiosity on tap. This curiosity, too, plays a prime role. The child is actively curious, just as he is actively active. He is forever wanting to know something, about anything and everything that crosses his path. The author remembers five-year-old David with wry amusement. "Hey," he inquired one day on his ump-teenth trip back from the bathroom, "how come *you* never have to go?"

This interest, this activity, this curiosity are actually allies of the learning process. They are indispensable to the learning process. The young child's repeated, vigorous forays into his expanding environment furnish the raw materials which he gradually fashions into concepts or generalized understandings.

Children start their learning *in utero* as well as from the first few minutes of actual birth. Evidence suggests that the newborn infant can discriminate forms in the early days of life and seems to prefer to look at more complex and interesting stimuli.[21] The young child's eagerness for learning is a characteristic. It is also a resource we cannot afford to ignore. Given the right conditions, he learns as naturally as he breathes.

Social Experience and Personality

When is the child's personality formed? Research provides support that individual differences in basic personality attributes are fairly well established by the age of six.[22] As Emmerich concluded, however, ". . . the findings do not indicate that traits are completely formed during early childhood. Also . . . even though a general personality trend may be established quite early, the manner in which it is expressed, indeed whether it is expressed directly at all, may continue to be quite susceptible to change."[23]

Zigler cautioned that we must view the child as an acting, thinking agent, a motivated organism who is not indiscriminately buffeted about by any wayward wind of experience.[24]

We are not dealing with an empty organism whom we may actually deprive or satiate through some simple experimental procedure. Rather, we are dealing with a programmed organism who, although open to change, maintains an integrity or consistency in his interactions with his social world.[25]

This social world is highly influential in shaping his responses to his environment. We have massive evidence which makes it clear that a child's social experience is a very influential factor in his development.[26]

Piaget believes that social interaction among children tends to correct the tendency to take an egocentric view of the world.[27] They may also learn more readily from a peer or a somewhat older child than from an adult whose views are more distant.[28]

Young children often imitate others as a source of learning. This may work to the advantage or disadvantage of the child, as mothers and teachers have long known. Research, too, indicates that when a model is provided, patterns of behavior are acquired rapidly in their entirety or in large segments.[29]

Bandura summarized experiments devised to determine the effect of real life and film-mediated or televised aggressive models.[30] He noted that exposure to aggressive models heightens children's aggressive responses to subsequent frustration, and these models are highly influential in shaping the form of their behavior.[31] This should give us pause in terms of the models our children view daily on their television and movie screens. The power this viewing has over their behavior is not surprising when we consider that imitative behavior in general is characteristic of young children.

> The findings that film-mediated models are as effective as real-life models in eliciting and transmitting aggressive responses indicates that televised models may serve as important sources of behavior and can no longer be ignored in conceptualizations of personality development. With further advances in mass media and audio-visual technology, models presented pictorially, mainly through television, are likely to play an increasingly influential role in shaping personality patterns and in modifying attitudes and social norms.[32]

All the more reason for a careful screening of the child's contacts with the mass media of comunication!

Nature versus Nurture

A controversy which has been raging for centuries is that between the adherents of heredity as the inhibiting factor in the attainment of an individual's full capacity and those of environment as the determining factor. It promises to be a continuing battle, and one with no definite victory for either side. For who can say where one begins and the other ends? It is like that brow-wrinkling riddle of the ages—which came first, chicken or egg?

To detail the lines of argument, according to the predeterminists, heredity is most influential, and the child, by implication, needs mainly room to grow according to his built-in design. This design is laid down before birth and development follows a fixed path. Preformationists insist that the blueprint of development is already fully detailed in sperm and ovum. The environmentalists believe that much, if not all, is possible through the proper environment, including the stimulation of the growth of children's mental development to new heights. They are proponents of the concept of plasticity in human intellectual development, which has given rise to intervention research. Zigler called it the "environmental mystique" with its plug for intelligence as an environmental product.[33] This environmental mystique, he asserts, is currently sweeping the country. He objects to the naïve acceptance of the view that all differences in cognitive functioning are due solely to differences in environmental input.

To consider a few high points in relation to current intervention research, Rosenzweig, Krech, and Bennett found in working with experimental rats that certain chemicals in the brain were associated with intelligence in rats.[34] Krech remarked:

> Finally in another series of experiments, we have demonstrated that these structural and chemical changes are the signs of a "good" brain. That is, we have shown that either through early rat-type Head Start programs or through selected breeding programs, we can increase the weight and density of the rat's cortex and its acetylocholinesterase and cholinesterase activity levels. And when we do—by either method—we have created superior problem-solving animals . . . I see a whole new area of collaboration in basic research between the educator, the psychologist, and the neurobiochemist.[35]

Bloom's study on environmental effects delineated:

1. Loss of development in one period cannot be fully recovered in another period.
2. Extreme environments can have far greater effects in early years of development. (The first four years are the most rapid period of growth. This period accounts for 50 percent of the child's intellectual development before age four.)

3. When a child moved from a deprived environment to a more abundant environment it was possible for many of them to increase their I.Q. as much as twenty points. . .[36]

Tumin provocatively asserted, "I don't doubt for one moment that a genuine revolution . . . would occur in public education in America and in every other country in the world if, in fact, education were to proceed on the simple and verifiable assumption that one can never know any child's ceilings or horizons of capacity if one continuously treats the child as a set of open possibilities."[37] The next step in this emphasis upon manipulation of the environment to maximize growth appears in Bruno Bettelheim's comments in the *New York Review of Books:* "This means that if we want to raise the intelligence of children by the possible maximum . . . we must change their environment long before they come of school age. To do this we will have to free ourselves of a few of our most widely held prejudices—that the child is the private property of his parents to do with as they please, that we are therefore powerless to change the environment he grows up in, and that human beings are infinitely improvable at any age, no matter what the home environment of their childhood."[38]

These are thought-provoking, strong statements. A modification of these either-or conflicting viewpoints was expressed by Zigler: "How a child will experience any particular environmental configuration can in part be objectively assessed by gauging both the level of cognitive development and the gross experiential history of the child prior to his encounter with this particular configuration."[39] Piaget's position, one that seems to express a middle-of-the-road approach, is detailed by Hunt as follows:

Piaget's conception of organism-environment interaction through assimilation and accommodation is neither hereditarian nor is it environmentalistic; it is both. . . . In any given situation, the first response of the child is one of those behavioral structures (schemata) already present from past assimilation. What variations in the environment do is to force the child to cope with this variation, and, in the coping, to modify the structures. This latter is accommodation, and the modifications are then assimilated through repetition in practice play.[40]

The possibility that children may be stimulated to reach hitherto unheard-of heights in development does exist. *Homo sapiens* has not reached the potential of which he is capable, by far. It has not been conclusively proven, however, that environment is solely responsible

for the gains in development which have been empirically demonstrated. In fact, there is no strong evidence as yet which suggests that
environment can change intelligence. The belief that if a child is
given the right materials and gadgets he can be turned into an above-
average learner is unduly optimistic. We must be realistic in our expectations of children or pessimism may be the result, with consequent regression in our budding programs for young children.

In spite of all the *Sturm und Drang* connected with intelligence in
this twentieth century, we actually know very little about the exact
nature of cognitive development. What is being stated currently is
that whatever it is that concerned, aware, middle-class parents are
doing for their children seems to be working, and we ought to be
doing it for all children.

Jeffrey, the son of a university professor father and anthropologist
mother, is an example of both genotype and phenotype in interaction
—that is, heredity and a stimulating environment. "I think you ought
to read *Oliver Twist* by Charles Dickens to the children sometime,"
he announced to his kindergarten teacher. "That's one of my favorites.
My mother reads a chapter to me every night."

"Tell us who Dickens is, Jeffrey," encouraged his teacher.

"He's an author who lived long ago and wrote many books. I
saw his house when we visited England this summer."

"Do you remember any of the other books he wrote?" He remembered a few, and then his teacher interjected, "*The Christmas Story*
is my favorite."

"I think you mean *The Christmas Carol*."

He was right, of course. This tactful correction coming from an
intelligent, alert five-year-old would do justice to a high school student.
He had the enriched home environment that we wish all children could
experience.

A kindergarten teacher in a government-sponsored Migrant Project gave the author the following vivid description of the thirty-two
children she taught, eighteen in the morning program, and fourteen
in the afternoon.

> Only a handful of them sleep in a bed and of these only two
> have beds of their own. One child has a private room, he sleeps in a
> closet. The average number of children in the family of these chil-
> dren is six. One child has sixteen children in his family and both
> parents are unemployable. Having made home visits I found as
> many as eight people sleeping in one room with perhaps only one
> cot for the parents to sleep on. The children sleep on the floor. On

these visits I found the children very reticent and apparently afraid to speak. One purpose of these visits was to obtain written permission for the children to go on field trips. I found that many of the parents cannot even write their names and sisters and brothers have to sign the slips. Most of these children have only one parent, a mother, and several have only a grandmother to raise them as they are already orphans at the age of five. One of my girls has a bullet wound in her thigh where a man shot her accidentally while trying to shoot her sister. Her mother died by a bullet wound and she has no father. The health of these children is appalling. Most of them are severely fatigued, have impetigo, worms and baby teeth that are already decayed beyond repair. Their poor health is greatly based on their diet which consists mostly of pork fat and beans, rice, Koolade, cokes and candy.

It is a combination of influences which help to shape the Jeffreys, the Marys, the Juans, the Susans, the Joes. These influences include both hereditarian and environmental factors. It is this combination which helps to shape and civilize the child.

Summary

The following contrasting points of view have been presented: (1) the notion of predetermined development which implies that a child should be allowed choice in the educative environment in terms of needs and interests, that he will find his level, and that he will develop in accordance with an inborn pattern and schedule; (2) the belief that the learning experiences of the child can be facilitated, and that the full expansion of his intellectual capacity is possible through a stimulating environment.

The point of view most promising in its implications for educators implies that appropriate educational experiences for young children are extremely important in and of themselves. However, there has been no evidence to date to show that these experiences can cause limitless cognitive growth. It would be well to use the contentions of the predeterminists—that is, consideration of children's present levels of growth and development in relation to the experiences offered to them in the school environment—as a sane point of departure.

NUTRITION AND THE GROWTH OF INTELLIGENCE

Vital Information

It is not only interesting but vital to consider our children's diets. What they ingest may make the difference between a healthy, active, curious, intelligent child and an underdeveloped, malnourished, dull child. This is an area of inquiry that has been too long neglected by the professional and lay public, with tragic results for sizable segments of our child population.

It is a sad truth that we cannot hope to accomplish the goals we want for our children in their brave new world of the future if we ignore their very real, present physical needs. A modern, well-planned educational facility filled with the best human and technological resources cannot stimulate the intellectual development of children who constantly live a marginal or semimarginal existence in terms of nutrition. In fact, the budding capabilities these children may have developed will be lost to our society. This is a costly waste for any society concerned with the optimal development of its individual citizens. Teachers who may reply defensively that they cannot be concerned about all kinds of needs, that they are in school to teach, are reminded that teaching is a complex endeavor, both art and science. And pupils do not roll into a classroom with only their heads, leaving the rest of their bodies outside.

A kindergarten teacher shared the following episode with the author:

> My first real awareness of the severe effect lack of food can have on a child was demonstrated to me by a four-and-a-half year old during my first few days of teaching. The children were lined up getting a drink of water next to the boys' bathroom. In front of the door to the bathroom were the remains of a cookie which had become almost unrecognizable by the dozens of feet that crushed it upon entrance and exit from the lavatory. One of my boys, a child who often caused disturbances in the class, spied the crumbs and made a mad dash to consume them. He got on the cold cement floor on his hands and knees and shoved the by-now black cookie remains into his mouth.

Need? Why, of course. If basic physiological needs are not being met, how can a child be expected to behave or learn in an acceptable manner? Notice that the teacher referred to the boy in that episode as a child who often caused disturbances. In an article concerned with nutrition and intelligence, the important point was made that poor nutrition results in not only poor physical appearance, but also poor behavior reactions in school activities.[41] It was no wonder that the boy reacted as he did. The wonder was that he was able to function at all.

Quality and Quantity

This was in a low socioeconomic area, and the problem was compounded by both lack of sufficient quantity of food as well as quality. If there is sufficient quantity, but it consists mainly of "filler" type food, such as bread, cake, pastries, soft drinks, then a serious problem still exists. The infant, toddler, and early-childhood youngster must have a diet that is high in protein since he needs more protein per pound of body weight than the adult. His diet should also be abundant in fruits and vegetables. If he does not receive these vital nutritional requirements during these critical, formative years of growth, his intellectual growth will be stunted, and the damage to his cognitive development will be quite possibly irremedial. In fact, there is empirical evidence that the first three months *in utero*, when the mother may not yet know that she is pregnant, is perhaps the most critical period of all. Matta explained:

> The first trimester is the most significant one since it is the period of organogenesis, or the formation of organs. In relation to the learning potential of the future child, the most rapidly growing organ is the brain and nervous system. Any factor affecting brain formation at this stage will leave an indelible scar which will translate into limitations of learning and resulting abnormal behavior. One can safely say that any condition affecting brain growth and development at this point will seriously affect learning.[12]

Role of Nutrition

A review of pertinent research indicates that we are slowly advancing in our empirical understandings regarding development and the role of nutrition.

> It is evident now that each individual is endowed with a given genetic potential for optimum physical and mental development. The ability of the individual to cope with his environment will determine his ability to realize his potentials. It is evident also that the nutritional ecology of the pre-school child is of prime importance in determining whether he will in fact realize his genetic potential.[43]

Investigators in this area point to infant and preschool nutrition as the key to human progress. Matta states that good nutrition is a prerequisite to the normal physical, mental, social and emotional growth and development of man.[44] In the conference proceedings organized under the auspices of the Committee on Protein Malnutrition and the Committee on Child Nutrition of the National Academy of Sciences Research Council, the following is emphasized: "Malnutrition in the preschool child is one of the world's most serious problems. . . . Not only is it killing and maiming the children of today, but also, through physical, mental and emotional damage, it will handicap the society of 1984, the next generation."[45] It is Barnes's contention that studies with experimental animals have demonstrated early malnutrition impairs learning behavior.[46] This confirms the general conclusion drawn from measurements of children. The effects of malnutrition on mental development in the early childhood period may be more severe and long lasting than its effects upon physical growth.

However, as is too often the case, we lag far behind in our practices. The problem is not confined to low socioeconomic areas, although it is perhaps aggravated there. Secretary of Agriculture Orville L. Freeman noted the results of a survey conducted by the U.S. State Department of Agriculture. According to this survey, one U.S. family in five lives on a diet termed nutritionally "poor," with a strong shift away from milk and milk products, fruits and vegetables to menus larded with baked goods and washed down with soft drinks. It is interesting to note that households from every socioeconomic income level turned up in the "nutritionally poor" category. He concluded, ". . . many Americans are making a poor choice—nutritionally —of our food abundance, and that to a large extent income does not determine good nutrition."[47]

A conference on malnutrition retardation highlighted findings which indicate that it is during the period when the human brain has its most rapid growth that intelligence may be irreversibly impaired due to malnutrition. During this rapid growth period of the brain, it reaches 80 percent of adult size. This occurs during the first three years of life![48]

Summary

Matta summarized the importance of nutritional ecology during the child's developmental years when he commented that the amount of physical activity and the food intake a child has during his formative years can alter his ability to fulfill his genetic potential.[49] All of us who work with children and parents have a responsibility to keep ourselves as well as others aware and informed about the critical nature of the young child's nutritional needs. If we are to succeed in helping the child to develop his potential, we must enlarge our narrow scope of concern. School plant, personnel, materials and equipment are necessary to any educational program. But if the learners are at half-mast in their efforts due to neglect of their vital physical needs, we have failed indeed.

NOTES

[1]L. Joseph Stone and Joseph Church, *Childhood and Adolescence* (New York: Random House, Inc., 1957), p. 144.

[2]J. McVicker Hunt, "The Psychological Basis for Using Preschool Enrichment as an Antidote for Cultural Deprivation," in Fred M. Hechinger (ed.), *Preschool Education Today* (New York: Doubleday and Company, Inc., 1966), p. 25.

[3]J. P. Scott, "Critical Periods in Behavioral Development," *Science*, Vol. 138 (1962), pp. 949–955.

[4]John Amos Comenius, *The School of Infancy*, edited by Ernest M. Eller (Chapel Hill: University of North Carolina Press, 1956), p. 69.

[5]*Ibid.*, p. 115.

[6]Fred M. Hechinger, "Passport to Equality," in Fred M. Hechinger (ed.), *Pre-School Education Today* (New York: Doubleday and Company, Inc., 1966), p. 9. Reprinted by permission of Doubleday and Company, Inc.

[7]Stone and Church, *op. cit.*, p. 142.

[8]David G. Kyle, "How Child Growth and Development Knowledge Makes a Difference," *Childhood Education*, Vol. 44 (January 1968), p. 283.

[9]*Ibid.*, p. 283–284.

[10]Edward Zigler, "Intellectual Development vs. the Whole Child," Address at the Annual Conference of the Southern Association on Children Under Six, Birmingham, Alabama, April 20, 1968.

[11]Myrtle M. Imhoff, *Early Elementary Education* (New York: Appleton-Century-Crofts, Inc., 1959), p. 49.

[12]John Kendrick Bangs, "The Little Elf."

[13]J. McVicker Hunt, *Intelligence and Experience* (New York: The Ronald Press Company, 1961), p. 272.

[14]United States Department of Health, Education and Welfare, *Functional Schools for Young Children*, Special Publication No. 8, Office of Education (Washington, D.C.: Government Printing Office, 1961), p. 7.

[15]Virginia M. Axline, *Dibs: In Search of Self* (Boston: Houghton Mifflin Company, 1964), prologue, p. xiii.

[16]Allen Bobroff, "The Stages of Maturation in Socialized Thinking and in the Ego Development of Two Groups of Children," *Child Development*, No. 31 (1960), p. 337.

[17]Elizabeth Mechem Fuller, *About the Kindergarten* (Washington, D.C.: National Education Association, February 1961), p. 6.

[18]*Ibid.*, p. 6.

[19]*Hunt, op. cit.*, p. 259.

[20]*Ibid.*, p. 259.

[21]R. L. Fantz, "Pattern Vision in Newborn Infants," *Science*, Vol. 140 (1963), pp. 296–297.

[22]Walter Emmerich, "Stability and Change in Early Personality Development," in Willard W. Hartup and Nancy L. Smothergill (eds.), *The Young Child* (Wash-

ington, D.C.: National Association for Education of Young Children, 1967), p. 252.

²³*Ibid.*, p. 253.

²⁴Edward Zigler, "Social Reinforcement, Environment, and the Child," *The American Journal of Orthopsychiatry*, Vol. 33 (July 1963), p. 620.

²⁵*Ibid.*, p. 620.

²⁶Martin Deutsch, "Facilitating Development in the Pre-School Child: Social and Psychological Perspectives," *Merrill-Palmer Quarterly of Behavior and Development*, Vol. 10 (July 1964).

²⁷Millie Almy, with Edward Chittenden and Paula Miller, *Young Children's Thinking* (New York: Columbia University Press, 1966) p. 138.

²⁸*Ibid.*, p. 138.

²⁹Albert Bandura, "Social Learning Through Imitation," in M. R. Jones (ed.), *Nebraska Symposium on Motivation* (Lincoln: University of Nebraska Press, 1962), pp. 211–269.

³⁰Albert Bandura, "The Role of Modeling Processes in Personality Development," in Willard Hartup and Nancy Smothergill (eds.), *The Young Child* (Washington, D.C.: National Association on Education of Young Children, 1967), p. 44.

³¹*Ibid.*, pp. 44–45.

³²*Ibid.*, p. 47.

³³Zigler, "Intellectual Development vs. the Whole Child," Address at the Annual Conference of the Southern Association on Children Under Six, Birmingham, Alabama, April 20, 1968.

³⁴M. R. Rosenzweig, D. Krech, E. L. Bennett, "A Search for Relations Between Brain Chemistry and Behavior," *Psychological Bulletin*, Vol. 57 (1960), pp. 476–492.

³⁵David Krech, "The Chemistry of Learning," *Saturday Review*, January 20, 1968, pp. 50, 68.© 1968 Saturday Review, Inc.

³⁶Benjamin Bloom, *Stability and Change in Human Characteristics*, (New York: John Wiley and Sons, 1964) in "We Had a Head Start on Head Start," *Young Children*, Vol. 21 (May 1966), p. 260.

³⁷Melvin Tumin, "The Emerging Social Policy in the Education of Young Children," *Young Children*, Vol. 23 (January 1968), p. 138.

³⁸Bruno Bettelheim, *New York Review of Books*, September 10, 1964, in *Journal of Research and Development in Education*, No. 3 (Spring 1968), p. 11.

³⁹Edward Zigler, "Social Reinforcement, Environment and the Child," *The American Journal of Orthopsychiatry*, Vol. 33 (July 1963), p. 615.

⁴⁰*Hunt, op. cit.*, p. 258.

⁴¹Sister William Marie, O.P. (Dominican Sisters), "Nutrition and Intelligence," *Catholic School Journal*, Vol. 64 (1964), pp. 45–46.

⁴²E. L. Matta, Jr., M.D., *Health, Learning and Behavior*, unpublished mimeo, November 1967, p. 8.

⁴³Philip L. White, "Nutrition and Genetic Potential," Highlights from address given to American School Health Association, A.M.A., Chicago, Ill., October 16, 1965, p. 1.

⁴⁴Matta, *op. cit.*, p. 34.

⁴⁵National Academy of Sciences-National Research Council, *Preschool Child Malnutrition, Primary Deterrent to Human Progress* (Washington, D.C.: National Academy of Sciences, 1966), General Summary.

⁴⁶Richard H. Barnes, "Some Effects of Nutritional Deprivations in Early Life Upon Learning Behavior, Nutrition and Mental Development," *The American Diatetic Association*, October 1966.

⁴⁷*Today's Child*, Vol. 16 (March 1968), p. 1.

⁴⁸Nutritional Foundation of New York and Massachusetts Institute of Technology, Conference on Malnutrition Retardation, *Pediatric News*, Vol. 1 (May 1967).

⁴⁹Matta, *op.cit.*, p. 51.

Chapter 2

How They Learn

COGNITIVE DEVELOPMENT

Growth of the Intellect

Jean Piaget and his colleagues at the Rousseau Institute in Geneva, Switzerland have made momentous contributions to our understandings concerning the growth and development of children's cognition. Due to his pioneer research, there is more awareness now that the child advances through a series of stages or sequences in the development of his intellect, as well as in physical, social and emotional aspects of growth.

Recent research on children's thinking generally confirms Piaget's view that young children's mode of reasoning and experience of reality are different from that of adults. These differences are not due to young children's ignorance, or lack of control over wishes and fears, or lack of proper teaching.[1] Piaget emphasized, "we wish to adapt teaching to the findings of developmental psychology as opposed to the logical bias of scholastic tradition."[2] As one of the outstanding figures in contemporary psychology, Piaget has evolved a general theory of intellectual growth which has, or should have, far-reaching implications for curriculum, methodology, and education in general. As Berlyne has noted, Piaget's ideas are closely tied to observation of behavior. This makes them the kind of psychology which can move science forward, since it is testable by reference to the facts of behavior.[3]

Since Piaget's writings are sometimes difficult for the novice to comprehend, even in translation, authorities such as Hunt, Flavell, and Almy have rendered a service by interpreting his work.

What are his outstanding contributions? Piaget, according to Hunt, has clarified better than anyone else the nature of the child-environment interaction during development.[4] Dual processes are at work during this interaction of child with environment. Accommodation by the child to the environment and consequent assimilation of information gained during this accommodation are both in operation during the child-environment interaction. And it is from this interaction that knowledge occurs.

Almy described it thus:

> The child is born with receptors that bring him information initially meaningless, about the sights, the sounds, the tastes of the world around him. Similarly, he is endowed with motor equipment that soon enables him not only to focus visually but even to turn his head toward an object, a face, a sound. Gradually his hands follow the lead of his eyes and impressions from visual and auditory modalities are coordinated with tactual information.[5]

In tracing this development of intelligence, she noted, "he may be regarded as storing information in patterns of action. . . . What a child assimilates, what gets incorporated into the repertoire of action patterns in part depends on the patterns he has already available. . . . New patterns do not emerge full blown and perfect."[6] This describes what Piaget calls sensori-motor schemata which develop throughout the period of infancy—the first eighteen months to two years of life. As detailed by Piaget:

> In other words, sensori-motor intelligence acts as a slow motion film, in which all the pictures are seen in succession but without fusion, and so without the continuous vision necessary for understanding the whole. . . .
>
> An act of sensori-motor intelligence leads only to practical satisfaction, i.e., to the success of the action, and not to knowledge as such. It does not aim at explanation or classification or taking note of facts for their own sake; it links causally and classifies and takes note of facts only in relation to a subjective goal which is foreign to the pursuit of truth. Sensori-motor intelligence is thus an intelligence in action and in no way reflective.
>
> As regards to its scope, sensori-motor intelligence deals only with real entities . . . it never concerns anything but responses actually carried out and real objects.[7]

The sequence of cognitive stages through which the developing child passes mark his progress toward an intellectual Mount Olympus. At the summit he finally attains understanding of abstract ideas and can deal comfortably with verbal propositions. This is the highest level of adult thinking, the stage of formal operations, and begins at the inception of adolescence—about eleven, twelve, or thirteen years of age. It is during adolescence, then, that thinking gradually becomes detached from concrete manipulation of actual objects and situations within the environment.

Almy recounts in an amusing aside that Piaget is said to have remarked that the immediate question of Americans, upon hearing about some process of development is, "How can you accelerate it?"[8] It seems that our penchant for speed is recognized on an international scale!

The dynamic elements in Piaget's approach which explain intellectual growth are assimilation and accommodation. Berlyne stated that Piaget

> . . . sees adaptation as an interplay of two complementary processes, which he calls "assimilation" and "accommodation." Assimilation occurs when an organism uses something in its environment for some activity which is already part of its repertoire. At the physiological level, it is exemplified by the ingestion of food, and, at the psychological level, it embraces a variety of phenomena. . . . Accommodation . . . means the addition of new activities to an organism's repertoire or the modification of old activities in response to the impact of environmental events. . . .
> As the child's development proceeds, a more and more complete balance and synthesis between assimilation and accommodation is achieved. The child is able to take account of stimuli more and more remote from him in space and time, and to resort to more and more composite and indirect methods of solving problems.[9]

The child's ability to benefit from adult instruction, it appears, is limited in the preoperational or intuitive thought stage. As Bruner explained:

> What is principally lacking . . . is what the Geneva School has called the concept of reversibility. When the shape of an object is changed, as when one changes the shape of a ball of plasticene, the preoperational child cannot grasp the idea that it can be brought back readily to its original state. Because of this fundamental lack the child cannot understand certain fundamental ideas that lie at the basis of mathematics and physics. . . . It goes without saying that teachers are severly limited in transmitting concepts to a child at this stage, even in a highly intuitive manner.[10]

Flavell clarified, "every instruction from without presupposes a construction from within."[11] However, this does not imply abdication from his role as guide and mediator on the part of the teacher. Rather, the importance of readiness is underlined and the matching of the encounters the child has with his environment in terms of what he is able to comprehend at his level of development. It is this matching which is the nucleus, and which breathes new life into that much verbalized but rarely practiced concept in educational circles: start where the child is!

Satisfaction of present needs and interests is generally considered important in the child's encounters with his environment. Evidence points to the existence of children's interests and these interests are considered a valuable resource for the educative process. Objections to interests as a resource are sometimes raised. This is generally due to the interpretation that provision for children's needs may be a limiting factor in program development. There is no real problem here. Satisfaction of present needs and interests should be accorded its rightful place in our educational schemes for the early childhood years, as well as stimulation of new interests, of new vistas.

Almy traced cognitive development in the following description:

> Once he has begun to use language, the infant, now a toddler, enters a new stage of development, during which his ways of thinking become progressively more like those of the adult. . . .
> Just as the child's encounters with his environment in the sensori-motor period led him to the discovery of the constancy of objects, so in the period of "concrete operations" he comes to the discovery of the invariance, or constancy of an increasing number of *aspects* of objects.[12]

She underlined the importance of the link between language and thinking in stressing that, "Perhaps the point to be made for those who would construct curriculum is that in the early childhood period activity and language need close association."[13] Piaget continued, "After the appearance of language, or, more precisely, the symbolic function that makes its acquisition possible (1½–2 years), there begins a period which lasts until nearly 4 years and sees the development of a symbolic and preconceptual thought."[14]

In continuing to trace the child's developing awareness of his environment, Piaget's studies demonstrated that:

> In the beginning school years, the young child perceives the world egocentrically and does not understand physical causality. At six or seven years of age the child has no true concept of time and space, of geographical relations, of past and future.[15]

As delineated by Piaget himself:

> From 4 to about 7 or 8 years, there is developed, as a closely linked continuation of the previous stage, an intuitive thought

whose progressive articulations lead to the threshhold of the operation.

From 7–8 to 11–12 years "concrete operations" are organized, i.e., operational groupings of thought concerning objects that can be manipulated or known through the senses.

Finally, from 11–12 years and during adolescence, formal thought is perfected and its groupings characterize the completion of reflective intelligence.[16]

"According to Piaget," Boehm indicated, "the young school child is still egocentric. . . . To him it means that the child is not yet able to distinguish fully between himself and the rest of the world–people or things. . . ."[17] Piaget said, "Thought, springing from action, is indeed egocentric at first for exactly the same reasons as sensori-motor intelligence is at first centered on the particular perceptions or movements from which it arises."[18] The preschool child, according to his studies, is essentially prelogical. He does not critically or logically examine evidence. A proposition is significant in proportion to how it directly affects him.[19]

He found in studying children's thought over thirty years ago that egocentric thinking in regard to concrete materials or problems which the child could solve by handling objects started to decrease at about the age of eight years. Piaget and his staff currently believe that this egocentric thought may be outgrown by modern children earlier than in the past because of their exposure to many more experiences through improved teaching methods and the mass media of communication.[20] Inhelder, a colleague of Piaget's, noted, too, that the age of the stages can vary with the nature of both the individual's experience and his hereditary potential.[21]

Concerning the stages of sensori-motor and concrete operations, Almy explained Piaget's theory thus: "The turning point comes for most children around the ages of seven or eight years. Consequently it is appropriate to regard the early childhood years, encompassing nursery school, kindergarten, first and second grades, as the years when thought is in transition between sensorimotor and concrete operations."[22]

Even when the stage of concrete operations is attained and is in force up to about eleven or twelve years of age, the child's reasoning is still linked to action.

Boehm, in interpreting Piaget, emphasized:

The child needs to look at objects. He needs to handle them. The younger the child, the more he learns through his senses. The infant learns to distinguish one thing from another by tasting, by touching, by smelling. The older child learns to distinguish by handling objects. Problems that he can solve by experimenting, he may not be able to solve on the verbal—that is, the abstract—level of thought. At ten and eleven the child thinks logically about fairly simple concrete matters even without experimentation. . . .

Gradually, the child learns to distinguish between himself and the world, between his ideas and those of others. He gains insight into the perspective of others and realizes that his perceptions and evaluations are subjective. He "depersonalizes" the world and recognizes that many events are fortuitous. According to Piaget, reality is now "dissubstantialized."[23]

Piaget highlighted the importance of physical activity and social interactions as necessary ingredients to experience. And experience, in turn, is always necessary for intellectual, or cognitive, development.[24]

Almy defined the meaning of this experience in terms of children's learning:

Piaget's theory leaves no question as to the importance of learning through activity. Demonstrations, pictured illustrations, particularly for the youngest children, clearly involve the child less meaningfully than do his own manipulation and his own experimentation. While the vicarious is certainly not to be ruled out, it is direct experience that is the avenue to knowledge and logical ability.[25]

In commenting on the implications for early childhood education of Piaget's theory and that of American investigators influenced by him and his colleagues, Burgess summarized the following principles:

1. The importance of sensorimotor experience is underlined.
2. Language, especially that which relates to labeling, categorizing, and expressing, is intimately tied to developing greater facility in thinking.
3. New experiences are more readily assimilated when built on the familiar.
4. Repeated exposure to a thing or an idea in different contexts contributes to the clarity and flexibility of a growing concept of the thing or idea.
5. Accelerated learning of abstract concepts without sufficient related direct experience may result in symbols without meaning.[26]

Hunt, too, stressed that during the phase of concrete operations, it appears important for the development of the intellect to provide opportunities to cope with a variety of materials, objects and gadgets.[27] In other words, concrete materials are a requirement for the child's thought operations. Hence the name, concrete operations.

Concept Formation

"It's green, it's green!" shouted the small figure clad in a paint-smudged smock who was diligently working on a large sheet of paper at the easel.

"What happened, Chipper?" questioned the other three- and four-year-olds in the nursery group.

His earnest face showed his excitement when he announced his discovery. "Look, it's green but I don't have a green color! I put the yellow and blue brush together. An' looka! It's green!"

This was obviously a significant moment for Chipper, and quite possibly a learning experience for his friends as well. The birth of a concept was underway: when one mixes two different colors, in this case blue and yellow, another color appears. Will it happen again? Will it happen with all kinds of mixtures? Will the color be green everytime? Repeated approaches over a period of time are entailed before the pieces begin to fall into place some kind of enduring picture emerges.

Fascinating learnings occur constantly among these explorative, questioning, curiosity-ridden early childhood youngsters. "You know what?" queried breathless four-year-old Mary. She had rushed between and around groups of children to get to the author with her special announcement that afternoon.

"What?"

"Humpty Dumpty wasn't a man. He was a egg!"

A milestone indeed. One wonders at the steps leading to this kind of comprehension. One also wonders what kind of help to give little Mike who announced very seriously, "My plant is growing. Does that mean it is born?"

Is it enough to explain, to simply tell Mike the difference between growth and birth? He will surely accept what teacher says because he looks up to her. And she can save a lot of "wasted time" by telling him straight out how things stand. But if she is cognizant of the child's level of mental development she will hesitate before this trap of glib, empty verbalization. She will realize that much more than words are needed for true comprehension. Torrance clarified:

> ... the weight of present evidence indicates that man fundamentally prefers to learn in creative ways—by exploring, manipulating, questioning, experimenting, risking, testing, and modifying ideas. Teachers generally have insisted that it is more economical to learn by authority. Recent research suggests that many things, though

The early childhood youngster is experience-bent.

not all, can be learned more effectively and economically in creative ways rather than by authority.[28]

According to a report of action research, young children do employ the essential elements of the process of concept formation—that is, associating ideas, attempting to discover cause and effect relationships, classifying and generalizing about things in the environment.[29]

What are concepts and how do they develop? Darrow explained that concepts may concern tangibles such as mother and boat or semitangibles such as love or cooperation. Concepts pertain to the phenomena, events and objects with which the child becomes familiar. She stated that concepts make up his thoughts, ideas, feelings, impressions, understandings, and views.[30] Kenneth Wann defined them as generalized ideas or understandings which embody many images or memories.[31]

Gardner stressed that concept formation occurs by means of repeated experiences with people, objects, situations and events.[32] Concerning developmental trends in concept formation, Russell commented that many American psychologists have been critical of Piaget's descriptive labels. They have not been able to verify his specific stages. They do, however, accept more general developmental trends from "a sensori-motor level, to a concrete perceptual level, to some sort of functional level, and finally to an abstract, conceptual level."[33] Bruner warned, "avoid premature symbolization. Do not give them the word to parrot before they know what it is about either by manipulation or in images."[34] That was Mike's difficulty. He was just parroting the words growth and birth without any real understanding of their meanings.

How can experiences be blended into a meaningful whole? Russell had this to say about integration: "Integration may take place during sensory impression, motor manipulation, questioning, reading, problem-solving, and creating. It may occur in relatively undirected patterns or in directed teaching."[35]

Concepts which may be visual, auditory or motor, appear to develop more fully and accurately if the child has a breadth of experiences. These experiences should include a wide variety of activities, concrete objects and materials, multisensory, problem-solving kinds of situations. And the more direct the experience, the better. Concepts, it appears, are the sine qua non, without which there is no true understanding. This is not to say, however, that children do not form misconceptions, or that they do not constantly need to rework and revise existing concepts in the light of new experiences. They do. So, too, do we. This incorporating of the new to existing "schemata," is at the heart of learning.

Children's misconceptions are the source of much information as well as amusement to the observant, alert adult. Their use of language can serve as an index to the accuracy of their concepts. "Snowball" is a case in point. Among the discernible differences between Snowball and the rest of the kindergarten class was the fact that Snowball had been retained in this kindergarten for two years. Also, he (she, it) was a rabbit who created a problem because no one knew this furry animal's gender. In no other way was this affectionate rabbit a problem. Joining in the activities at the block corner, during snack time, and hopping from center-of-interest to center-of-interest were favorite occupations, particularly at the easel corner, housekeeping area, and library nook. Finally, the teacher became upset at her own inability to discern Snowball's true sex, and determined to enlist a parent resource for help. The resource in question was a pediatrician and the father of one of the morning group's youngsters. He obligingly came, and to the children's delight, he carefully checked Snowball's state of health with the aid of instruments from his black bag. Also, incidentally, he checked his gender.

"You have a fine, healthy rabbit," he announced to the waiting group. "A girl rabbit."

Since this was the morning group, the teacher carefully relayed the health bulletin to the afternoon youngsters when they arrived. And added, "Snowball is a girl."

"I knew it, I knew it," shrieked Sheila.

"You did?" her astonished teacher asked. "How?"

"Because she has such long fingernails!" replied Sheila triumphantly.

A child's-eye-view of the weather and another misconception was provided by one kindergarten boy when his teacher asked him, "Why does it snow? What causes it to snow?"

"God listens to the weather forecast and makes it snow," he explained.

Jeff provided his capable kindergarten teacher with an important clue to his concept and language development in a group discussion one day. She had just finished reading a story to the rapt youngsters about some animals and their humorous adventures. They discussed the kind of animals, how many there were, and what happened to them. The actual sequence of events was skillfully drawn from the children, and then the teacher asked, "What kind of a story would you call this?"

Jeff replied, "It was a laughable one."

"You can think of a better word to use than that, Jeff," prodded his teacher.

A momentary pause, and then he responded, "O.K. How's ludicrous?"

An excellent word, indeed, for any five-year-old! The wise teacher will use clues such as the one Jeff provided in helping her to determine the kinds of experiences for which individual children may be ready. Since Jeff had already given her many such clues, she decided to furnish him with some individualized reading instruction geared to his interests.

Gardner summarized the ingredients which are an integral part of concept formation:

> Thus it still comes back to utilizing his own personal experience as the basis for developing concepts, even though the concepts may enable him to go, mentally, beyond the narrow bounds of his specific experience. The child's ability to form useful concepts is not only a reflection of his level of mental development, it is a direct aid in his intellectual growth, with meaningful concepts serving as the basis for the development of other, additional concepts. One builds on the foundation of others. . . .
>
> The general process of concept formation moves from the concrete, tangible, and specific toward the more general, less tangible, and more abstract.[36]

Summary

Concepts are the nucleus of a child's thinking process. They represent his attempts to organize his own personal environmental experiences into relationships invested with meaning for him. Concepts can be formed, clarified and extended by provision for direct experiences, multisensory impressions, motor manipulation, problem solving, creating and questioning. Through involvement in the following types of activities, young children's early beginnings of concept formation will grow in fertile ground:

1. Discussions, demonstrations, observations, experiments, and exhibits.
2. Constructions, murals, paintings, drawings, and other art media.
3. Dioramas, globes, felt books, gadget boxes.
4. Puppets, dramatization, role playing, and play activities.
5. Scrap books, experience booklets, and experience-language charts.
6. Books, stories, illustrations, panorama of pictures.
7. Music, recordings, dances, games, and rhythms.
8. Celebrations and holidays.
9. Trips, visitors, and other community resources.
10. Concrete objects and artifacts from our country and abroad.
11. Audio-visual materials—films, filmstrips, tapes, television, photographs.

ROLE OF PLAY

What Is It?

When one asks a child what he did at his school all morning, or all afternoon, the by-now classic reply will likely be: "Oh, we just played." Or, the infinitely worse rejoinder, "Nothing."

It is quite true that, in the strictest sense, many of the activities in the early childhood school could be considered play. The child does play. But it is not "just play." In fact, it has been said that play is the work of children. This is literally true. It is a fun way to learn, but it is serious business, too. This is the classic way that the young of the species have discovered the world around them throughout the ages, in the play way natural to the early years.

Centuries ago when children were considered to be just like adults, only smaller, this was frowned upon. It was also actively beaten out of the youngsters since play was considered a sign of depravity, of evil, of sin. It smacked of the devil himself. As we became more enlightened and less superstitious, as we learned more about children and how they grow and develop, we stopped believing this foolishness.

At times, however, there are signs that we are reverting to the days of old, back to the foolishness based on fear, superstition, and lack of knowledge. Also, it is a regression to a very utilitarian view that what is useful to survival is considered important in direct proportion to its contribution to this survival. At these times an expression may be heard which seems to be a favorite, "Let's get these children down to business." Ironically, play is their business.

The role of play in the growth and development of the child has been given significance which seems to vary according to the investigator's own special area of interest. Smith described it thus:

> In classical psychoanalytic and Piagetian theory, the play of the child is said to have mainly compensatory function. For the analyst, play has little significance for intellectual growth except as it helps to reduce the amount of tension that might be impeding intellectual activity somewhere else. . . . Several generations of sociologists . . . have seen play as providing model situations in which the child rehearses roles he will later occupy seriously somewhere else. While most of these sociologists emphasize the social value of play, some also stress cognitive implications.[37]

Erikson stated that the child uses play in order to gain mastery over his environment, while the adult uses it as a "vacation from reality."[38] For Piaget, the child who plays is actually getting to know and deal with his environment. He described symbolic play or imaginative play as the purest form of egocentric and symbolic thought.[39]

Lieberman noted that there are frequent references in the literature which suggest that a playful attitude is necessary in divergent thinking.[40] She found a significant relationship between playfulness and ability on several creative tasks.[41] "With the growing emphasis on divergent thinking or creativity, it is imperative to investigate what factors might influence and foster this type of thinking."[42] She asserted that both the kindergartner and the adolescent represent important age points in relation to identification and encouragement of divergent thinking. "In the preschool years one might say that spontaneity flows uncensored by the logical operations that mature after eleven."[43]

Insights Gained

Examples of this spontaneity in early childhood groups are numerous. So, too, are the thoughtful insights which may be gained by the listening, watchful adult, insights which will be reflected in the kinds of guidance and activities we provide for children.

Scene: A group of fours sitting at low tables and eating a family-style lunch in an early childhood setting. (The following conversation was recorded by the author, who incidentally forgot to eat in her consuming interest over this spontaneous, fascinating dialogue.)

Nancy to student teacher sitting at the head of this table for six, "Anita, do you still have that baby in your tummy?"

The sound of a gulp, as Anita quickly swallowed her food and then carefully replied, "I never did have one, Nancy."

"First you are a seed," offered David.

"Yes," piped up a serious-faced redhead, "A seed, then a baby, then a people."

"No, you are a baby," insisted Nancy.

"First you are a seed," the redhead maintained.

"Everybody has to die," offered another.

"Yep," said David with a satisfied air of one who puts the final piece in the puzzle. "First a seed, then a baby, then you are big, you get old, and die."

Score one for family-style lunches eaten in the homelike atmosphere of the early childhood room, rather than in an antiseptic, large, jarring cafeteria. There is much incidental learning possible in such a setting, for adults as well as children!

Why Play?

Isaacs observed play episodes of young children over a period of years in an English nursery school, and these observations and interpretations provide a fruitful source of "total responses of children to whole situations," since, "partial studies of this or that response to limited experimental problems may be no more than sterile and misleading artifacts."[44] Observation in unstructured as well as structured situations is still the best way for the sensitive, knowledgeable, understanding adult to learn about children.

The value of play as an activity was reaffirmed by Olson: "Play creates many practical situations in which the child discovers and observes, and reasons and solves problems."[45]

Hartley, Frank and Goldenson, who wrote the most complete analysis of children's play and its potentialities both for understanding young children and encouraging their development, emphasized the importance of

> . . . creative activities and play opportunities within preschool and early school settings. . . . What is perhaps not so frequently emphasized is the great plasticity of the young during these years, their

instant response to environmental impacts, their relative freedom from compartmentalization, and their consequent readiness to benefit from favorable experiences and to assimilate these into their growing concept of self.[46]

They distinguished eight functions which dramatic play serves in ages 3–5½ years:

1. To imitate adults.
2. To play out real life roles in an intense way.
3. To reflect relationships and experiences.
4. To express pressing needs.
5. To release unacceptable impulses.
6. To reverse roles usually taken.
7. To mirror growth.
8. To work out problems and experiment with solutions.[47]

The importance of play to the child's cognitive development was emphasized by Lewis:

> The importance of imaginative play in a child's cognitive development is that it readily expands into exploratory and constructive play which, as it presents him with successive problems, demands the exercise of reasoning. . . . For instance, in playing with water, he explores its physical properties and is confronted with problems which he may try to solve.
>
> In the growth of this exploratory and experimental play, language may play a part of ever-increasing importance. . . . . He verbalizes his own acts, and so aids his perception, helps his recall of relevant past experience, helps his imaginative constructions, his anticipations and predictions and so fosters his conceptual and generalized thinking in the direction of reasoning. . . . The effects of language are immeasurably reinforced as the child comes to play with others—particularly if adults take interest in what he is doing. Language then helps to make play more imaginative, more constructive and a greater stimulus to reasoning.[48]

Summary

It has been stated that play is the child's way of learning about the world. It is also the adult's best way to learn about the child and the many facets of his growth and development. Children reveal themselves in their play activities. There is much the astute observer can learn about a child's-eye-view of the world. Most adults lose their early receptivity to the world on the long, hard road to maturity.

Saint-Exupéry's delightful fairy tale for adults abounds with illustrations of our loss of contact with our youth and with the really essential parts of life and living:

Grown-ups love figures. When you tell them you have made a new friend, they never ask you any questions about essential matters. They never say to you, "What does his voice sound like? What games does he love best? Does he collect butterflies?" Instead, they demand: "How old is he? How many brothers has he? How much does he weigh? How much money does his father make?" Only from these figures do they think they have learned anything about him.

If you were to say to the grown-ups: "I saw a beautiful house made of rosy brick, with geraniums in the windows and doves on the roof," they would not be able to get any idea of that house at all. You would have to say to them: "I saw a house that cost $20,000." Then they would exclaim: "Oh, what a pretty house that is!"[49]

Yes, play is children's business. There must be genuine respect for the value of play as an integral part of the sound early childhood program. Surrounded by stimulating, growth-inducing materials and equipment, a sensitive, aware teacher, and a program based on understanding of child growth and development, these early childhood youngsters are "down to business." The best kind—for them.

SUGGESTED READINGS

Almy, Millie. *Child Development*. New York: Holt, Rinehart and Winston, Inc., 1955.

———, Edward Chittenden, and Paula Miller. *Young Children's Thinking*. New York: Columbia University Press, 1966.

Auleta, Michael S. (ed.). *Foundations of Early Childhood Education: Readings*. New York: Random House, Inc., 1969.

Ausubel, David Paul. *Theory and Problems of Child Development*. New York: Grune and Stratton, Inc., 1958.

Axline, Virginia M. *Dibs: In Search of Self*. Boston: Houghton Mifflin Company, 1964.

———. *Play Therapy*. Boston: Houghton Mifflin Company, 1947.

Baruch, Dorothy. *One Little Boy*. New York: Julian Press, Inc., 1952.

Bettelheim, Bruno. *Love Is Not Enough*. New York: Free Press, 1950.

Biber, Barbara. *Schooling as an Influence in Developing A Healthy Personality*. New York: Bank Street College Publication, 69 Bank Street.

———. *Play as a Growth Process*. New York: Bank Street College Publication, 69 Bank Street.

Bijou, Sidney W., and Donald M Baer. *Child Development II*. New York: Appleton-Century-Crofts, Inc., 1965.

Bloom, B. J. *Stability and Change in Human Characteristics*. New York: John Wiley and Sons, Inc. 1964.

Bossard, J. H. S., and E. S. Boll. *The Sociology of Child Development*. Third edition. New York: Harper and Row, Publishers, 1960.

Bowlby, John. *Child Care and the Growth of Love*. 2d ed. Baltimore: Penguin Books, 1965.

Breckenridge, Marian E., and Margaret N. Murphy. *Growth and Development of the Young Child*. Seventh edition. Philadelphia: W. B. Saunders, 1964.

Brisbane, Holly E., and Audrey P. Riker. *The Developing Child*. Illinois: Charles Bennett Co., Inc., 1965.

Bruner, Jerome S. *The Process of Education*. Cambridge: Harvard University Press, 1962.

Burton, W. H., and H. Hefferman. *The Step Beyond: Creativity*. Washington, D.C.: National Education Association, 1964.

Children's Bureau, U.S. Department of Health, Education and Welfare. *Your Child From 1 to 6*. Washington, D.C.: Superintendent of Documents, 1962.

Cohen, Dorothy H., and Virginia Steon. *Observing and Recording the Behavior of Young Children*. New York: Columbia University Press, 1958.

Crow, Lester D., and Alice Crow. *Child Development and Adjustment: A Study of Child Psychology*. New York: Macmillan Company, 1962.

Davis, John E. *Play and Mental Health*. New York: A. S. Barnes and Company, Inc., 1939.

D'Evelyn, Katherine. *Meeting Children's Emotional Needs, A Guide for Teachers*. Englewood Cliffs, N.J.: Prentice-Hall, Inc., 1957.

Dinkmeyer, Don C. *Child Development, The Emerging Self*. Englewood Cliffs, N.J.: Prentice-Hall, Inc., 1965.

Driscoll, Gertrude. *How to Study the Behavior of Children*. New York: Columbia University Press, 1941.

English, Horace. *Dynamics of Child Development*. New York: Holt, Rinehart and Winston, Inc., 1961.

Erikson, Erik H. *Childhood and Society.* Second edition. New York: W. W. Norton Company, Inc., 1963.

Flavell, J. H. *The Developmental Psychology of Jean Piaget.* Princeton: D. Van Nostrand Company, Inc., 1964.

Fowler, W. *Concept Learning in Early Childhood.* Washington, D.C.: National Association for Education of Young Children, 1965.

Frank, Lawrence K. *The Fundamental Needs of the Child.* New York: The National Association for Mental Health, Inc., 1952.

Freiburg, Selma. *The Magic Years.* New York: Charles Scribner's Sons, 1959.

Furth, Hans G. *Piaget & Knowledge: Theoretical Foundations.* Englewood Cliffs, N.J.: Prentice Hall, Inc., 1969.

Gardner, D. Bruce. *Development in Early Childhood—The Preschool Years.* New York: Harper and Row, Publishers, 1964.

Gesell, Arnold, and Frances L. Ilg. *Infant and Child in the Culture of Today.* New York: Harper and Brothers, 1943.

————. *The Child From Five to Ten.* New York: Harper and Brothers, 1946.

————. *The First Five Years of Life.* New York: Harper and Row, 1940.

Ginott, Haim. *Between Parent and Child.* New York: The Macmillan Company, 1968.

Ginzberg, E. (ed.). *The Nation's Children, Volume 2, Development and Education.* New York: Columbia University Press, 1960.

Gordon, Ira J. *Studying the Child in the School,* New York: John Wiley & Sons, Inc., 1966.

Greene, Margaret C. C. *Learning to Talk, A Parent's Guide for the First Five Years.* New York: Harper and Row, Publishers, 1960.

Griffiths, Ruth. *A Study of Imagination in Early Childhood and Its Function in Mental Development.* London: Routledge & Kegan Paul, Ltd., 1935.

Haeusserman, E. *Developmental Potential of Preschool Children: An Evaluation of Intellectual, Sensory and Emotional Functioning.* New York: Grune and Stratton, Inc., 1958.

Hartley, Ruth E., Lawrence K. Frank, and Robert M. Goldenson. *Understanding Children's Play.* New York: Columbia University Press, 1952.

Hartup, Willard W., and Nancy L. Smothergill. *The Young Child, Reviews of Research*. Washington, D.C.: National Association for Education of Young Children, 1967.

Havighurst, Robert J. *Developmental Tasks and Education*. Second Edition. Chicago: The University of Chicago Press, 1948.

————. *Human Development and Education*. New York: Longmans, Green and Company, 1953.

Hunt, J. McVicker. *Intelligence and Experience*. New York: Ronald Press Company, 1961.

Hymes, James L. Jr. *A Child Development Point of View*. Englewood Cliffs, N.J. Prentice-Hall, Inc., 1955.

Inhelder, Barbel, and Jean Piaget. *The Early Growth of Logic in the Child*. New York: Harper and Row, Publishers, 1964.

Isaacs, Nathan. *The Growth of Understanding in the Young Child* (Studies of Piaget). London: Ward Loche Educational Supply Association, 1964.

Isaacs, Susan. *Intellectual Growth in Young Children*. London: Routledge & Kegan Paul, Ltd., 1930.

————. *Social Development in Young Children*. London: Routledge & Kegan Paul, Ltd., 1933.

————. *The Children We Teach*. London: University of London Press, Ltd., 1950.

————. *The Nursery Years*. London: Routledge & Kegan Paul, Ltd., 1932.

Jersild, Arthur T. *Child Psychology*. 5th ed. Englewood Cliffs, N.J.: Prentice-Hall, Inc., 1960.

Kagan, J., and H. Moss. *Birth to Maturity*. New York: John Wiley and Sons, Inc., 1962.

Kepler, Hazel. *The Child and His Play*. New York: Funk and Wagnall Company, Inc., 1952.

Kuhlen, Raymond G., and George G. Thompson. *Psychological Studies of Human Development*. New York: Meredith Publishing Company, 1963.

Lambert, Clara. *Play, A Yardstick for Growth*. New York: Play School Association, 120 West 57th Street.

Landreth, Catherine. *The Psychology of Early Childhood*. New York: Alfred A. Knopf, Inc., 1962.

————. *Early Childhood Behavior & Learning.* New York: Alfred A. Knopf, Inc., 1967.

Lanford, Louise. *Guidance of the Young Child.* New York: John Wiley and Sons, 1960.

Lawrence, Evelyn, et al. *Some Aspects of Piaget's Work.* London: National Froebel Foundation, 1964.

Lowenfeld, Viktor. *Creative and Mental Growth.* Third edition. New York: The Macmillan Company, 1957.

Moustakas, Clark E. *Children in Play Therapy.* New York: McGraw-Hill Book Company, 1953.

————. *Psychotherapy With Children: The Living Relationship.* New York: Harper and Brothers, 1959.

Murphy, Lois Barclay. *The Widening World of Childhood.* New York: Basic Books, Inc., 1962.

————, et al. *Personality of the Young Child.* Volume II. New York: Basic Books, Inc., 1956.

Mussen, Paul H., and John J. Conger. *Child Development and Personality.* New York: Harper and Brothers, 1956.

Piaget, Jean. *The Child's Conception of Number.* New York: Humanities, 1952.

————. *The Child's Conception of Physical Casuality.* London: Routledge & Kegan Paul, Ltd., 1930.

————. *The Child's Conception of the World.* London: Routledge & Kegan Paul, Ltd., 1951.

————. *The Construction of Reality in the Child.* New York: Basic Books, Inc., 1954.

————. *Judgment and Reasoning in the Child.* New York: Harcourt, Brace and Company, 1928.

————. *The Language and Thought of the Child.* New York: Harcourt, Brace and Company, 1926.

————. *The Moral Judgment of the Child.* London: Routledge & Kegan Paul, Ltd., 1932.

————. *The Origins of Intelligence in Children.* New York: International Universities Press, Inc., 1952.

————. *Plays, Dreams and Imitation in Childhood.* New York: W. W. Norton and Company, Inc., 1962.

_____. *The Psychology of Intelligence.* New York: Harcourt, Brace and Company, 1950.

_____, Inhelder, Barbel, and A. Szeminska. *The Child's Conception of Geometry.* New York: Basic Books, Inc., 1960.

Pitcher, Evelyn, et al. *Helping Young Children Learn.* Columbus, Ohio: Robert Merrill Company, 1966.

Rasey, Marie, and J. W. Menge. *What We Learn From Children.* New York: Harper and Brothers, 1956.

Redl, Fritz. *Understanding Children's Behavior.* New York: Columbia University Press, 1954.

Reeves, Katherine. *Children . . . Their Ways and Wants.* Connecticut: The Educational Publishing Corporation, 1959.

Ridenour, Nina, and Isabel Johnson. *Some Special Problems of Children: Aged 2 to 5 Years.* New York: National Association for Mental Health, Inc., 1960.

Ritchie, Oscar W., and Marvin R. Koller. *Sociology of Childhood.* New York: Appleton-Century-Crofts Company, Inc., 1964.

Russell, David H. *Children's Thinking.* Boston: Ginn and Company, 1956.

Saint-Exupéry, Antoine de. *The Little Prince.* New York: Harcourt, Brace & World, Inc., 1943.

Stendler, C. B. *Readings in Child Development and Behavior.* Second edition. New York: Harcourt, Brace & World, Inc., 1965.

Stephens, Ada. *Providing Developmental Experiences for Young Children.* New York: Columbia University Press, 1952.

Stone, Joseph L., and Joseph Church. *Childhood and Adolescence.* Second edition. New York: Random House, Inc., 1968.

Strang, Ruth. *Helping Children Solve Problems.* Better Living Booklet No. 522. Chicago, Ill.: Science Research Associates, 1960.

Torrance, E. Paul. *Creativity.* Washington, D.C.: Department of Classroom Teachers, American Educational Research Association of the National Education Association, 1963.

Vygotsky, L. S. *Thought and Language.* New York: John Wiley and Sons, Inc., 1962.

Wallach, Michael A., and Nathan Kogan. *Modes of Thinking in Young Children.* New York: Holt, Rinehart and Winston, Inc., 1965.

Wann, Kenneth, Miriam S. Dorn, and Elizabeth A. Liddle. *Fostering Intellectual Development in Young Children.* New York: Columbia University Press, 1962.

Witmer, Helen, and Ruth Kotinsky. *Personality in the Making.* New York: Harper & Row, Publishers, 1952.

Wolf, Anna, and Suzanne Szass. *Helping Your Child's Emotional Growth.* New York: Doubleday and Company, Inc., 1954.

Wolff, Werner. *Personality of the Pre-School Child.* New York: Grune and Stratton Company, 1946.

Young, Leontine. *Life Among The Giants.* New York: McGraw-Hill Book Company, 1965.

NOTES

[1]Charles D. Smock, "Children's Conception of Reality: Some Implications for Education," *Journal of Research and Development in Education* Vol. 1 (Spring 1968), p. 35.

[2]Jean Piaget, *Psychology of Intelligence* (Paterson, N.J.: Littlefield, Adams and Company, 1963), p. 146.

[3]D. E. Berlyne, "Recent Developments in Piaget's Work," *British Journal of Education Psychology,* Vol. 27, 1957, in Robert Harper, et al. (eds.), *The Cognitive Processes* (Englewood Cliffs, N.Y.: Prentice-Hall, Inc., 1964), p. 322.

[4]J. McVicker Hunt, *Intelligence and Experience* (New York: The Ronald Press Company, 1961), p. 259.

[5]Millie Almy, "New Views on Intellectual Development: A Renaissance for Early Childhood Education," unpublished mimeo, in Evangeline Burgess, *Values in Early Childhood* Education (Washington, C.D.: National Education Association, 1965), p. 33.

[6]Millie Almy, "New Views on Intellectual Development in Early Childhood Education," in *Intellectual Development; Another Look* (Washington, D.C.: Association for Supervision and Curriculum Development, 1964), p. 15.

[7]Jean Piaget, *The Psychology of Intelligence,* translated by M. Percy and D. E. Berlyne (London: Routledge & Kegan Paul, Ltd., 1950), in William Kesson and George Mandlen (eds.), *The Child* (New York: John Wiley and Sons, Inc., 1965), pp. 275–276.

[8]Millie Almy, with Edward Chittenden and Paula Miller, *Young Children's Thinking* (New York: Columbia University Press, 1966), p. 42.

[9]Berlyne, *op. cit.,* pp. 311–312.

[10]Jerome S. Bruner, *The Process of Education* (Cambridge: Harvard University Press, 1960), pp. 34–35.

[11]J. H. Flavell, *The Developmental Psychology of Jean Piaget* (Princeton: D. Van Nostrand Company, Inc., 1963), p. 406.

[12]Millie Almy, "New Views on Intellectual Development: A Renaissance for Early Childhood Education," unpublished mimeo, 1963, in Evangeline Burgess, *Values in Early Childhood Education* (Washington, D.C.: National Education Association, 1965), pp. 33–34.

[13]Millie Almy with Edward Chittenden and Paul Miller, *Young Children's Thinking* (New York: Columbia University Press, 1966), p. 138.

[14]Piaget, *op. cit.,* p. 277.

[15]Leonore Boehm, "Exploring Children's Thinking," *The Elementary School Journal*, No. 61 (April 1961), pp. 370–371.

[16]Piaget, *op. cit.*, p. 278.

[17]Boehm, *op. cit.*, p. 363.

[18]Piaget, *op. cit.*, p. 277.

[19]Jean Piaget, *The Language and Thought of the Child* (New York: Harcourt, Brace and Company, 1926).

[20]Boehm, *op. cit.*, p. 365.

[21]Barbel Inhelder, "Criteria of the Stages of Mental Development," in J. M. Tanner and Barbel Inhelder (eds.), *Discussions on Child Development* (New York: International University Press, 1953), pp. 75–85.

[22]Millie Almy, "New Views on Intellectual Development in Early Childhood Education," *Intellectual Development; Another Look* (Washington, D.C.: Association for Supervision and Curriculum Development, 1964), p. 20.

[23]Boehm, *op. cit.*, p. 365.

[24]Jean Piaget, "Cognitive Development in Children: The Piaget Papers," in R. E. Ripple and V. N. Rockcastle (eds.), *Piaget Rediscovered: A Report of the Conference on Cognitive Studies and Curriculum Development* (Ithaca: Cornell University Press, 1964).

[25]Millie Almy, with Edward Chittenden and Paula Miller, *Young Children's Thinking* (New York: Columbia University Press, 1966), p. 137.

[26]Evangeline Burgess, *Values in Early Childhood Education* (Washington, D.C.: National Education Association, 1965), p. 35.

[27]Hunt, *op. cit.*, p. 281.

[28]E. Paul Torrance, *Creativity* (Washington, D.C.: American Educational Research Association, National Educational Association, July 1965), pp. 12–13.

[29]Kenneth D. Wann, Miriam S. Dorn, and Elizabeth A. Liddle, *Fostering Intellectual Development in Young Children* (New York: Columbia University Press, 1963), p. 19.

[30]Helen Fisher Darrow, "Research: Children's Concepts." *Childhood Education*, Vol. 60 (January 1964), pp. 247–254.

[31]Wann, Dorn and Liddle, *op. cit.*, p. 12.

[32]D. Bruce Gardner, *Development in Early Childhood: The Preschool Years* (New York: Harper & Row Publishers, 1964), p. 216.

[33]David H. Russell, "Concepts," *Encyclopedia of Education Research* (Third Edition, New York: The Macmillan Company, 1960), p. 329.

[34]Jerome S. Brunner, "Needed: A Theory of Instruction," in *Educational Leadership* (Washington, D.C.: National Education Association, May 1963), p. 530.

[35]Russell, *op. cit.*, p. 329.

[36]Gardner, *op. cit.*, pp. 216–217.

[37]Brian Sutton-Smith, "The Role of Play in Cognitive Development" in Willard W. Hartup and Nancy L. Smothergill (eds.), *The Young Child* (Washington, D.C.: National Association for Education of Young Children, 1967), pp. 99–100.

[38]Erik H. Erikson, *Childhood and Society* (New York: W. W. Norton & Company, Inc., 1950), pp. 185–190.

[39]Jean Piaget, *Play, Dreams and Imitation in Childhood* (London: Routledge & Kegan Paul, Ltd., 1951).

[40]J. Nina Lieberman, "A Developmental Analysis of Playfulness as a Clue to Cognitive Style," *The Journal of Creative Behavior*, Vol. 1 (Fall 1967), p. 395.

[41]J. Nina Lieberman, "Playfulness and Divergent Thinking: An Investigation of Their Relationship at the Kindergarten Level," *Journal of Genetic Psychology*, Vol. 107 (1965), pp. 219–224.

[42]J. Nina Lieberman, "A Developmental Analysis of Playfulness as a Clue to Cognitive Style," *op. cit.*, p. 395.

[43]Ibid., p. 395.

[44]Susan Isaacs, *Social Development in Young Children* (London: George Routledge & Sons, Ltd., 1933), p. 4.

[45]Willard C. Olson, *Child Development* (Second Edition, Boston: D. C. Heath and Company, 1959), p. 49.

[46]Ruth E. Hartley, Lawrence K. Frank and Robert M. Goldenson, *Understanding Children's Play* (New York: Columbia University Press, 1952), p. 4.

[47]*Ibid.*, pp. 27–28.

[48]M. M. Lewis, *Language, Thought and Personality* (New York: Basic Books, Inc., 1963), p. 126.

[49]Antoine de Saint Exupéry, *The Little Prince* (New York: Harcourt, Brace and Company, 1943), pp. 17–18.

Part II

Concerns for the Thoughtful

Chapter 3

Childhood Past and Present

ROOTS OF EARLY CHILDHOOD EDUCATION

No complete agreement exists, or has ever existed, as to the nature of the optimum environment for the young child or any age child. This is not surprising. Unless we find a way to turn out people who are as alike as proverbial peas in a pod in their views on what is important and what is not, we will never have accord about either the nature or means of attaining the good life or about helping our young to reach this summit.

Our educational backgrounds and experiences, as well as personal philosophy, adjustment to life, goals and ambitions are part and parcel of all we do for and with children. They enter into how we see our roles in relation to the nurturance of our young.

There is general agreement now about the tremendous consequence of the periods of growth and development contained in infancy, toddlerhood, preschool and the middle years of childhood as well as adolescence. In fact, we have made giant strides as a civilization in our common recognition of the child as father of the man. There is even a nagging realization now that we had better look to this child for hopes of any metamorphosis within our time.

It was not always thus. Childhood is a fairly recent "discovery" dating back to the turn of this twentieth century.

The superintendent of the State of Georgia presented a paper at the annual meeting of the National Education Association in which he highlighted the importance he attached to this discovery of the child. This occurred in the year 1900.

> If I were asked what is to be accounted the great discovery of this century, I would pass by all the splendid achievements that men have wrought in wood and stone and iron and brass. I would not go to the volume that catalogs the printing-press, the loom, the

steam-engine, the steamship, the ocean cable, the telegraph, the wireless telegraphy, the telephone, the phonograph. I would not go among the stars and point to either one of the planets that have been added to our solar system. I would not call for the Roentgen ray that promises to revolutionize the study of the human brain as well as the human body. I would pass over all the labor-saving machines and devices by which the work of the world has been marvelously multiplied. Above and beyond all these the index finger of the world's progress, in the march of time, would point unerringly to the little child as the one great discovery of the century now speeding to its close.[1]

A Brief History of the Preschool

The extension of education downward to include young children and upward to include higher education and adult education is a phenomena of the twentieth century. Early childhood education as it exists today did not appear full blown. It reflects the influence of leading men and women: the philosophers, educators, psychologists, anthropologists, psychiatrists, pediatricians, sociologists, scientists, and philanthropists of the past and present. It reflects the sociological, economic, and even political climate within a culture. It reflects the standards and ethics of that culture.

The early elementary education of the child began in the home. In fact, the family was the most important educational agency among all early peoples.[2] During various eras of history, there was acknowledgment that community effort was needed to supplement family training. The community intruded upon, or was enlisted by, the family in its traditional task of educating its young.

In ancient civilizations, organized schooling usually began anywhere from age seven to ten. The Hebrews were an exception to this, since their children were taught at home until the age of six. In medieval times, the Saracens had universal, free elementary education for their youngsters from the age of five to eight.[3]

The community in these and other instances not only suggested or prescribed an education appropriate for the offspring, but also often held the power of life and death over these offspring.

> Now the character of this education and the position of the child in the family group has at any given time been very largely influenced by the attitude of contemporary society toward the rights and duties of the child as an individual. This attitude varies greatly at different times and in different places. . . .[4]

Early Education in Europe

The neglect of little children was the main reason for the establishment of schools for early education on the continent.[5] Another reason was that parents weren't able to take proper care of their children due to hard work, and, in many cases, incompetency.[6]

The early infant school is the common origin of both the kindergarten and nursery school, and it was frankly philanthropic in purpose. Infant school practice changed through the influence of various educational leaders. Among the men who struggled for reform and who profoundly affected the early infant school, and later the kindergarten are Comenius, Rousseau, Oberlin, Owen, Pestalozzi, and Froebel.

John Amos Comenius, a Moravian bishop who lived in the seventeenth century, influenced the development of the theory and practice of early education by his writings. He was the first modern theorist to fully appreciate the importance of training the child from birth.

He stressed the importance of the child's play three centuries before it became significant in education:

> . . . parents ought to be especially careful never to allow their children to be without delights. . . . Let their spirits be stirred by happy play. . . .[7]
> Elders ought to assist by showing them the forms of all things, even of playthings (for they cannot yet be occupied in real works) and by playing with them.[8]

The child's need for activity, and the advantage of group experiences as part of the child's education also received attention from this man.

If a child's enthusiasm is aroused, he will want to learn, said Comenius. The child cannot be taught unless he is interested. Dewey restated this three centuries later when he stressed interest as a motivating factor in learning.

Forest summarized Comenius's contributions in the following statement:

> Because of the high value which he set upon the child's spontaneous activity and because of his interest in the preschool period, Comenius has been called "the father of the modern kindergarten."[9]

Jean Jacques Rousseau's ideas left an imprint on early education.

He was a proponent of the experience-centered curriculum, and stated in his influential book, *Émile:*

> As a general rule—never substitute the symbol for the thing signified, unless it is impossible to show the thing itself; for the child's attention is so taken up with the symbol that he will forget what it signifies.[10] . . .
> Let the senses be the only guide for the first workings of reason.[11]

The first duty of the educator, said he, is to study each individual child since each is different. Hence, how foolish to educate all in the same manner! Rousseau shared Comenius's belief that children were not miniature adults, but personalities in their own right.

His vivid writing enabled his ideas to receive a wide audience.

> Rousseau firmly established three great modern principles of teaching: (1) the principle of growth, (2) the principle of pupil-activity, (3) the principle of individualization—those basic principles that lay at the heart of all the pregnant reforms of Pestalozzi, Herbart, Froebel. . . .[12]

It remained for Pestalozzi, Froebel, and later Dewey to translate these ideas into practical theory and application.

Robert Owen is considered a main influence in the infant school movement. He established an infant school in 1790 in connection with the cotton mills which he managed in New Lanark, Scotland.

Following are the characteristics of his educational plan which were in contrast to the philanthropic undertakings of the day:

1. He was definitely hostile to religion.
2. He emphasized the importance of helping the child get acquainted with his environment; he would have him study "things," he would have him learn about animals, and plants, and trees.
3. In the Institute at New Lanark little children were taught to dance, and sing, and be joyous.
4. The philanthropist was, according to his way of thinking, mainly engaged in breaking the child's will and subduing a corrupt nature to the end that a self-respecting citizen, content in his station, might result. Owen was interested in consciously forming habits which would develop a nature fundamentally good, although limited in part by heredity, into the good moral character.[13]

Jean Frederic Oberlin founded knitting schools for little children in the Vosges mountains because, like Owen, he was interested in the young children of the poor. ". . . He in a sense anticipated the work of Froebel and Pestalozzi, using pictures, stories, manual training, and excursions as school activities."[14]

Johann Heinrich Pestalozzi's notion of "Anschauung" is similar to Comenius's belief that the educator should make full use of the child's senses in order for the child to learn best. Pestalozzi believed that the natural order of instruction was to begin with the impressions of the objects themselves, before any verbal instruction. He emphasized, as Comenius did, that education should begin at birth, and that mothers should be given definite suggestions as to how to instruct their children. Pestalozzi did not appreciate as fully the value of play for its own sake as Comenius and Froebel did, and looked upon it as gymnastic exercise. He realized the importance of the plasticity of the early years, as Comenius and Froebel did, was among the first to emphasize the importance of the teacher, and to advocate specific training for teachers. His teaching methods included concrete materials, cooperative procedures, thinking and doing. These methods influenced the teaching of children and the preparation of teachers to a great extent not only in his native Switzerland, but also in Prussia and later in the United States. He earned the title of "father of modern education."

Friedrich Wilhelm Froebel's contribution was the kindergarten, or the *Kleinkinderbeschäftigunganstalt* as it was originally named. Vandewalker asserted:

> According to Froebel, education must begin on the child's level, and with the material, intellectual or social, that has already acquired a meaning to him. . . . In the social sense, therefore, as well as in the intellectual, education is and must be, even from the beginning, a phase of life, not a preparation for it.[15]

He planned kindergartens for all classes, not just for the children of the poor. Unfortunately, Forebel's kindergartens were banned for a period of ten years by the reactionary Prussian government of that day. Froebel prophesized that in democratic America "the kindergarten would prosper as in no other country." His legacy is contained in the following list: (1) school should provide a rich, happy environment for children; (2) education is larger than books or formal drill; (3) the child's present interests and needs should be the basis of the curriculum, and creative self-activity should be the method; (4) play is the natural means of expression for the child at this level; (5) the spirit of cooperation and the group are both important to the child's social development; and (6) the aim of the kindergarten should be individual development. The effects of his principles are felt in the kindergarten and in the elementary school today.

The Kindergarten in the United States

The kindergarten idea was brought to the United States by German immigrants who fled after the unsuccessful revolution of 1848.

Mrs. Carl Schurz, a former student of Froebel, opened a kindergarten in Watertown, Wisconsin, in 1855. She taught her own children and the children of relatives in the Froebelian manner in this first kindergarten in the United States. She was instrumental in stimulating the interest and enthusiasm of Elizabeth Peabody in Froebel and the kindergarten when she visited Miss Peabody's city of Boston in 1859. Miss Peabody, the apostle of the Froebelian kindergarten in the United States, opened the first English-speaking kindergarten in Boston in 1860.

Other influences which helped the kindergarten in its period of introduction in the United States were as follows: (1) the European Revolution of 1848 which brought German immigrants to this country and resulted in their establishment of ten kindergartens before 1870; (2) the efforts made on behalf of the kindergarten by Henry Barnard, Elizabeth Peabody, Mrs. Horace Mann, Maria Bolte Kraus, John Kraus, Susan Pollock, William N. Hailman, Elizabeth Harrison, Susan E. Blow, William T. Harris, Kate Douglas Wiggin, Anna Bryan, Patty Smith Hill, Alice Temple, John Dewey, William Kilpatrick, G. Stanley Hall, and Francis Parker; (3) the model kindergarten which operated during the Philadelphia Exposition of 1876; (4) the endorsement of the kindergarten by the National Education Association in 1872; (5) the contributions of leading kindergarten educators in the form of articles, books, manuals, translations of German works, pamphlets, the publication of periodicals devoted to kindergarten education, and lectures; (6) the annual school reports of superintendents in cities which had adopted the kindergarten; (7) kindergarten associations, of which there were over 400 in 1897; (8) women's clubs; and (9) religious and philanthropic interests.

The attempts at modification of the established kindergarten procedure, as outlined by Froebel, were greeted with approval by some and disapproval by others. There was a temporary division in the ranks of the kindergarten professionals into conservatives and liberals. Elizabeth Peabody and Susan Blow were leaders of the conservative element. Patty Smith Hill and the other liberals allied themselves with the new psychology and the child study movement. As a result, the liberals won and the modern kindergarten of today no longer reflects the heavy symbolism, the gifts and occupations, and the symbolic games of the traditional Froebelian kindergarten. Vandewalker commented:

> The advent of the psychologist, therefore, marked a turning point in the history of the kindergarten movement. That movement could never have attained the influence that it now exerts in the educational world, however, without the sanction of psychology and child study.[16]

G. Stanley Hall is considered the father of the child study movement in America. This movement which began between 1880 and 1890 has had far-reaching effects upon the school. The child was studied and observed in order to determine the significant aspects of his growth and development. But this was not the only goal envisioned by Hall and his disciples. Hall's larger goal was embodied in an editorial in *The Pedagogical Seminary* in 1895:

> Back of all these and other educational problems, however, are the nature and needs of the growing child and youth, and the best sign of the times that the present educational awakening has struck deep root and that the near future will see greater advance than the recent past, is the fact that American teachers are slowly realizing that the only philosophic and even rational and consistent education is ultimately based solely on a knowledge of the growth of the body, brain, and soul of the young of the human species.[17]

Vandewalker highlighted the prevalent attitude toward the kindergarten in the years following the Chicago Exposition by indicating:

> The evidences of kindergarten progress which the exposition afforded were so unmistakable, the approval accorded that institution by the leading educators at the Educational Congresses was so marked, and the phases of education for which it stands were seen to be so clearly in line with the most progressive tendencies that even the most skeptical could not fail to be impressed.[18]

In summary, the impetus for the establishment of kindergartens in the United States was at first philosophic in nature, as it was on the continent. Its primary purpose now is educative.

Unfortunately, recognition of the value of education for this early childhood period has lagged. A goal of the kindergarten now is a goal which the primary grades had many years ago: recognition of the value of the kindergarten and universal incorporation of it as an integral part of public education for all four- and five-year-old children in the United States.

Harold Howe, U.S. Commissioner of Education, commented:

> As we learn more about the learning process, all indicators point to early childhood education as the option we most need to pick up. Laboratory schools, private and cooperative nurseries, day-care centers, early education for the handicapped—all have contributed a rich body of information on the behavior of four- and five-year-olds. We have welcomed research from these sources into the literature for almost 50 years, but only about three-fifths of America's children below age six have the chance for kindergarten, and the number attending school below age five remains negligible. . . .
>
> Powerful evidence indicates that the level of intellectual achievement is half determined by age four and another 30 percent is predictable at age seven. . . .
>
> I would predict that by the year 2000 most children in the United States will be attending regular public schools starting at age four. If things run true to form, the "experts" will still be arguing whether it is a good idea to start formal learning that early, but the new frontiers of the elementary school will then be among the three-year-olds, many of whom will be going to school at home on TV.[19]

Montessori and Early Childhood

There is a current resurgence of interest in Maria Montessori's methods and materials for the education of young children. The approaches devised by this nineteenth and early twentieth century psychiatrist were based upon her experiences with the mentally retarded in the clinics of Rome and her background studies of the theoretical framework provided by psychologists in the area of mental retardation—Itard and Seguin, for example. The structured methods and didactic materials designed by Montessori seemed to be effective in her clinic work with the mental "defectives" as they were labeled. The government of Rome permitted her to expand her "system" to the poor children of the crowded tenement areas of the city, since she strongly believed that all children would benefit from her work. Her schools gradually increased in number on the continent but did not become popular in the United States until after the advent of Sputnik. Montessori schools have capitalized upon the post-Sputnik climate with its increased demand for pupil achievement and academic skills. By the age of five or six, Montessori-trained children frequently are performing in the three R's—reading, 'riting,' and 'rithmetic. Her methods extend to the elementary grades, but Montessori schools generally enroll the early childhood age groups.

The underlying theme for the educational scheme planned by Montessori is auto-education—that is, self-education. The child freely selects from among the available sense-training materials, and learning is expected to occur during the interaction between child and materials. Experimentation, exploration or improvisation with the materials are not permitted. This interaction between child and material is a highly structured one, since a material may be used only in accordance with specific procedures and set sequences. Hence there is one acceptable way defined for each task within the Montessori approach, whether this task is to build a building, scrub a table surface, wash the hands, or wring out a cloth. The focus is upon children in relation to material, usually working alone with an object or objects. The responsibility for the child's learning leans heavily upon the proper use of these materials within the highly structured, carefully prepared environment.

Social interaction between children is not encouraged, nor is play considered an activity of any value. Montessori was quoted as saying that if she had believed in the value of play, she would have provided for it. Since play is not a part of her system, her opinion of it is quite clear. The conscious omissions of social interaction and play activities are serious in the light of new understandings we have concerning their contributions to the child's language development and concept formation as well as social, emotional, physical and mental growth and development.

The narrow scope allowed the Montessori teacher in the kinds of relationships which may be established with the children as individuals and as groups should be another area of concern to educators. The role of the teacher is a relatively passive one. It includes the dissemination of specific directions for the "exercises in daily living" and in the proper use of the sensory-discrimination materials. Beyond this task-orientation and a general concern for and emphasis upon discipline, there is a minimum of direct contact between teacher and child. Achievements by the child may or may not be acknowledged by the teacher, since this young learner is expected to be most motivated by his own inward sense of satisfaction in a job well done.

Interviews with two first-grade teachers who have had numerous opportunities to work with children from a variety of kindergartens were reported as follows:

> *Question:* Tell me about your Montessori children.
> *Teacher 1:* I can spot a Montessori child in my room before I have read any of his background information.
> They can't adjust to routine. They won't sit in one place. I have children right now who have been in school for three months who will not settle down to completing a written task. Montessori children are so independent . . . they intend to do just what they please.
> *Teacher 2:* I suppose the main fault I find with Montessori children is that they are so dependent on direction. When they have completed a given task, instead of looking at a book, or coloring a picture, they say, "What shall I do now?" "Tell me something to do."
> If I put a scrapbox out and tell the children to get busy and create anything they want, my Montessori children are just at a loss. They have no idea what to do with anything in the scrapbox. "What shall I do?" "How shall I make it?"

Beginning research in this area raises questions as to the long-range effects of a Montessori-type, rigidly structured program upon the development of divergent thinking and creativity within the young learner. Definitive research is needed in this area. In the broadest sense, there should be careful study in relation to the kinds of learning climates which are most conducive to the optimal development of the young child as a reacting, feeling, thinking, ongoing unit—not simply as a one-dimensional learner preparing for academic skills.

CURRENT CONCERNS

The crucial issue is summed up tersely by Hunt, "The problem for the management of child development is to find out how to govern the encounters that children have with their environments to foster both an optimally rapid rate of intellectual development and a satisfying life."[20] It is, perhaps, the underlying theme of the mid-twentieth century, this effort to maximize each child's growth to its highest potential. A worthy objective, but one receiving a variety of interpretations.

The Tigers in our Midst

Finding permanent solutions is difficult because shifting patterns, turmoil and instability are the order of the day. In a word: CHANGE.

*Satisfying aesthetic experiences which stress process
rather than end product.*

And now we are entering an age in which the mass media of communication will expand into giant octupuslike proportions, throwing tentacles into every facet of our daily existence. The Mc-Luhans in our midst have heralded its coming.

With this scene as the backdrop, a commitment made by a young nation looms as one of the most awe-inspiring challenges in the history of man. This commitment to present and future generations of children involves a tremendous concept never before attempted on such a grand scale: to educate all the children of all the people.

It is a monumental task at best. But, couple it with our current era during which we are experiencing both a population and information explosion, plus a race toward a new generation of super intellects which had the unleashing of Sputnik in 1957 as its trigger, and the picture emerges with frightening clarity: education with numerous tigers by the tail. Yet we are attempting to accomplish our monumental task to the accompaniment of cries of derision, handwringing, accolades and watchful eyes.

How can we deal successfully with these tigers? First and foremost, clear thinking and courage on the part of trained, talented educators is vitally needed.

Individuals such as Bruner present the challenging hypothesis "that any subject can be taught to any child in some honest form."[21] The corollary to his hypothesis is, "then it should follow that a curriculum ought to be built around the great issues, principles, and values that a society deems worthy of the continual concern of its members."[22]

There are provocative questions which pinpoint the dilemma in regard to teaching young children the "structures of knowledge," as proposed by Bruner & others, in order that these children achieve a conceptual framework at an early age. Fraser and Pullen asked these questions:

> Finally, even if the structures of a particular discipline can be agreed upon and it is proven that people can grasp them, there still remains the question of whether such study is the best use of pupils' time at their particular stage of development. Is there other learning that they need more at their age? Would they grasp the concepts and generalizations of the academic scholars more quickly and with more understanding at a later time?[23]

Moore's project on the cognitive processes of young children has created another kind of furor in educational circles. He presented evidence accumulated from thirty-five children, aged 2–5, who worked with special typewriters in a laboratory context in the New Haven area. After daily, controlled sessions in cubicles, each of which contained one of these electric typewriters, the children learned to type, to letter, to read, and to take dictation. "It is important to understand," emphasized the sociologist, "that the capacity to learn these skills at an early age is not unique to gifted children."[24]

This capacity is undoubtedly not unique to gifted children. Surely, homo sapiens would have no difficulty in attaining the skill aspect of reading, since animals in laboratory settings have been able to achieve a range of skills in a conditioned learning environment. It is well to consider that reading is more than a skill, however; it is more than mere word-calling. Comprehension is at its base. One wonders, also, if these twos, threes, fours and fives would be better off spending their time in active pursuit of a wide range of direct, firsthand environmental encounters. This is at the heart of concept formation, which is, in turn, at the heart of the child's growth in thinking and learning. Yet, claimed Boehm, " . . in many countries the curriculum and teaching methods fail to take this fact into consideration. School programs and teaching practice are not related closely enough to intellectual growth."[25]

As highlighted by the Symposium on Child Development, ever since the appearance of Sputnik, there has been a reversal of the trend to center education around the needs of the child as an individual rather than around society's needs as a society.[26] There is increasingly strong emphasis now upon "standards imposed from without, periodic checks and utilization of the individual child's resources for the benefit of society."[27] There is a very real danger that we may be losing sight of the child as a child. Under the guise of preparation for the future, we are inundating him in an avalanche of ever-increasing demands.

Our schools of today have been very much affected by these new demands created by the various forces in this post-Sputnik period. There are new pressures affecting our children. The current emphasis upon the learning of an ever-expanding quantity of subject matter is making itself felt down into the lower grades of the elementary school, kindergarten and nursery school levels. We are placing youngsters of all ages in hothouse, pressure-cooker environments intent upon forcing or hastening their growth through developmental stages in jig time. Now that we have finally discovered children, we seem to be trying for instant adults.

Another kind of conflict, or perhaps the same basic conflict in another dimension, has materialized. Opposing groups are marshalling their forces around a surge for excellence. One faction sees the child as a future citizen of a nation which has special requirements dictated by the times in which we live, and views the child mainly as an instrument to be fashioned by these special requirements. Others maintain that we have gained nothing if we lose sight of the individual and that any group, particularly in a democracy, is only as strong as its separate units, or members. This conflict is actually as old as the history of man and will no doubt continue as long as man exists on this planet. It has come into prominence again.

The question, "Whither are we going?" is receiving a variety of answers. Our younger generation seems to be well aware of the forces being shaped by the adults in their lives. A six-year-old in the author's first-grade class a few years ago knew what the score was and reacted accordingly. His goals did not happen to coincide with the author's goals for him, but were illuminating nevertheless. "Say," he began one morning in late autumn, "report cards are coming out pretty soon, aren't they?" The author agreed that, yes, this was the case. "Well then," he continued with a purpose, "my father said he'd give me a dollar for every 'A' I got." A momentary pause, then the memorable conclusion, "And you know what? I'll split with you!"

Whither are we going?

Help Offered

Our profession is receiving help from every quarter, solicited and otherwise. Big business seems to feel we are not competent to face the ever-increasing hordes of children who descend upon our classrooms every autumn. They offer help for our seeming incompetent and chaotic condition in the form of depersonalized gadgets and structures. The phenomenally rapid rise of the new educational technology is a reflection of their proposed solutions to our problems. This technology is reaching into every grade level of our educational continuum, including early childhood education. It is based upon the proposition that our children must learn ever more and machines will help them to cram in the facts. This is delaying the inevitable day of reckoning. Practical decisions must be made regarding this cramming process, since the information explosion shows no signs of abeyance, and is, in fact increasing.

Voices from another quarter offer a remedy in the form of statistical groupings, and claim that attention to individuals as such is a luxury we cannot afford. Scientists offer solutions arising from anti-septic laboratory environments, pointing with pride to pigeons and rats that perform amazing feats thanks to the stimulus-response-bond. Communities at large attribute their maladjusted members either to a lack of hickory sticks or hairbrushes in schools, or lack of tender loving care, depending on the whims of fashion.

The uproar we hear is due to the various pressures being exerted on our captive audience: our children.

The Time Is Now

It is time for us to stop moving with the ponderous pendulum. It is time for us to stop jumping on the most popular and/or noisiest bandwagon. It is time to start asking the right questions, as, for example, What do we believe in most and what data do we have to support these cherished beliefs? Does the research offered to us from a laboratory context work with live children in a classroom? What does it mean to us in the light of our experience with and understanding of children? How can we use it? What are the key ideas underlying the various subject-matter areas and how can these best be taught to the child? What are the present attitudes which our youngsters hold about the world at large and what can we do to change these if need be? How can we keep the world open and exciting for our children rather than uninteresting and stereotyped? Should our new emphases in curriculum reorganization and development be on new structures of departmentalization and specialization? Or should we be consider-ing questions such as the following: What are we doing to help develop independence, problem solving, values, thinking and under-standing of selves in our children? And, as a corollary, are these im-portant areas of concern for the school?

Where We Stand

It is time for us not only to start asking, but to start telling, too. It is time to say firmly to our critics: This I believe. The personal quality in teaching is more important now than ever before. Interpersonal relations should not be displaced by the new trend toward deper-sonalization. We deal with the sensitive human spirit, not with parts of an atom molecule, robot, or electric brain. Children do not roll into schoolrooms as disembodied heads. They come with their whole top-to-toe selves. Children can get excited pushing buttons. They can even acquire a set of skimpy concepts and facts by this method. But this is a small part of the total learning process. This does not take care of the intuitive grasp of ideas, of internalization, of understanding. We are interested in concept formation because it is basic to true understanding. And concept formation is a slow, gradual process based on much exploratory experiencing. We do not want to add to the world's already large supply of glib verbalizers. We are interested in growth, not regurgitation on cue. And growth is often intangible. We deal with intangibles. They cannot be added up in column formation in a ledger.

It is time for us to say to our critics: Believe in us. We welcome help from other disciplines. We are aware of the contributions which an interdisciplinary approach can offer to the problems besetting us. But we must sift, refine, and reconstruct in the light of our own background of experience with and understanding of children.

Our nation is as strong and vital as its individual units, or citizens. Let us not lose sight of our ultimate goal for the citizens of the future, our children: critical thinking arrived at through many experiences in problem-solving settings. The school we should be striving for has broadly conceived purposes for children that reflect a concern for them as individual human beings. In addition, all the physical as well as human resources of the community are used to present children with opportunities to learn in realistic settings. Lowell of Harvard expressed it well: "The real thing we want is not knowledge but resourcefulness."

The tigers can be tamed!

However, as long as a single child sits in a classroom anywhere with a strong feeling that he is just a cog in a giant system which engulfs him in the a.m. and spews him forth in the p.m., with a strong feeling that dismissal time represents relief and freedom, just so long are we demonstrating our failure to meet the new challenges in this latter part of the twentieth century. The challenges are there for all to see. They come at a time when more children than ever before sit in the classrooms of the nation, pass in and out of our schools in ever-increasing numbers each academic year. They are beginning to stretch in a long, arid line from kindergarten to senior university level.

Where can thoughtful educators turn for answers in the midst of new challenges, new problems, and controversy? To our court of first and last resort: the child. There must be increasing emphasis upon the need to pace children's growth during their formative years with learnings which are appropriate for the individual and for the group, and reflect concern for the individual child as a total responding whole. One of the outcomes which Piaget's work suggests is that the child tends to revert to the intuitive level when environmental demands are too heavy and removed from meaningful, concrete content. This child cannot cope when there is an inappropriate match between his developmental level and the experiences extended to him.

Whither are we going? A thoughtful, provoking reply to this question was offered in the keynote address to the National Conference of State Legislators:

> The class of 1984 will be stepping into an unbelievably exciting, but also a new kind of world. This new world will demand a new kind of person . . . a person with genuine flexibility and freedom, a person who thrives on sensing and solving problems as complex and subtle and new as the technological environment of tomorrow. In this new world, rigidity may actually be a greater barrier to progress than ignorance.
>
> In short, we can't presume to describe precisely the specifications of the "job" which needs to be done by tomorrow's leaders. But precisely in our inability to describe the job, I think we accurately describe the kind of men and women we need.[28]

NOTES

[1]G. R. Glenn, "What Manner of Child Shall This Be?" National Education Association, *Proceedings*, Vol. 1900, No. 39, pp. 176–178, in *Daedalus* (Summer 1962), p. 503.

[2]Elmer Harrison Wilds, *The Foundations of Modern Education* (New York: Farrar and Rinehart, Inc., 1936), p. 238.

[3]*Ibid.*, pp. 240–241.

[4]Ilse Forest, *Preschool Education; A Historical and Critical Study* (New York: The Macmillan Company, 1927), p. 2.

[5]*Ibid.*, p. 68.

[6]*Ibid.*, p. 72.

[7]John Amos Comenius, *The School of Infancy*, ed. Ernest M. Eller (Chapel Hill: University of North Carolina Press, 1956), p. 84.

[8]*Ibid.*, p. 91.

[9]Forest, *op. cit.*, p. 113.

[10]Jean Jacques Rousseau, *Émile*, translated by Barbara Foxley, Everyman's Library, quoted in Marjorie B. Smiley and John S. Diekhoff's *Prologue to Teaching* (New York: Oxford University Press, 1960), p. 372.

[11]*Ibid.*, p. 370.

[12]Wilds, *op. cit.*, p. 398.

[13]Forest, *op. cit.*, p. 60.

[14]*Ibid.*, p. 62.

[15]Nina C. Vandewalker, *The Kindergarten in American Education* (New York: The Macmillan Company, 1913), p. 249.

[16]Vandewalker, *op. cit.*, p. 244.

[17]G. Stanley Hall, editorial in *The Pedagogical Seminary*, 1895, quoted in Vandewalker, *op. cit.*, p. 237.

[18]Vandewalker, *op. cit.*, p. 246.

[19]Harold Howe II, U.S. Commissioner of Education, Department of Health, Education and Welfare, *Picking Up the Options*, unpublished mimeo, from an address, 1968, pp. 1–4.

[20]J. McVicker Hunt, *Intelligence and Experience* (New York: The Ronald Press Company, Inc., 1961), pp. 362–363.

[21]Jerome S. Bruner, *The Process of Education* (Cambridge: Harvard University Press, 1962), p. 52.

[22]*Ibid.*, p. 52.

[23]Dorothy McClure Fraser and Thomas G. Pullen, Jr., "What To Teach," *NEA Journal*, October 1962, p. 36.

[24]Omar K. Moore, *Orthographic Symbols and the Preschool Child—A New Approach* (University of Minnesota: Published in the proceedings of the Third Minnesota Conference on Gifted Children, October 1960), p. 1.

[25]Leonore Boehm, "Exploring Children's Thinking," *The Elementary School Journal*, No. 61 (April 1961), p. 363.

[26]Symposium, "Child Development Research: The Next Twenty-Five Years," *Child Development*, No. 31 (March 1960), p. 198.

[27]*Ibid.*, p. 198.

[28]Peter G. Peterson, "The Class of 1984 . . . Where Is It Going?," Keynote Address, National Conference of State Legislators (Washington, D.C.: National Committee for Support of the Public Schools, December 4, 1966), p. 17.

Chapter 4

Why Kindergarten?[1]

The five-year-old has come into new national prominence. As the former stepchild of educational programs and curricula, he now emerges as an important concern on the minds of many varied interest groups.

The cure for the ills of a host of educational, economic, and social diseases is now being sought in this tiny personage. These range from the high dropout rate in our secondary schools and colleges, and low reading, 'riting and 'rithmetic achievement of a whole new generation of pupils to the rising unemployment due to automation, and the lack of skilled labor.

What actually can be expected of this budding five-year-old? How does this school year, the kindergarten, fit into the scheme of things? Can it be and is it helpful in any way for the average five-year-old? Are any of the benefits lasting, and can they be traced in the later grades of the elementary school?

The kindergarten today is the product of its own rich past as well as the modern expression of a culture's determination and concern to provide its young with the best. The kindergarten is the leading proponent of the belief in education as a process of self-expression, and the belief that the character of early education should be determined by the child's growth and development. It stands for an attitude toward childhood which has not only influenced its own practices and procedures but also those of the other grades of the school.

It is difficult to single out one particular year of a child's life and point to it as being the most important. The culprit year, or the savior year. Growth and development are continuous. But certainly, a good year at any level is desirable for the child's overall success. Conversely, a poor year in which the child is deprived of learning opportunities in a rich environment is not desirable, either for his present development or his future success.

ACHIEVEMENTS

Can we measure what he has gained? Some research studies seem to suggest that the activities during the kindergarten year do have a directly measurable result. These studies point to greater achievement by the kindergarten-trained in the later grades of the school. This greater achievement is in the areas of reading, arithmetic, personality development, social adjustment, and adjustment in general. Others question that this achievement can be measured, or that it is perceivable in any concrete ways.

Educators are in agreement, however, that a good beginning is important. It is a year well spent, even though we may not be able to measure results directly. As yet, we cannot accurately or sensitively measure many learnings—learnings in attitudes, interests, appreciations, understandings, and even in skills. It is true that many tests and other measuring devices have been developed in the past fifty or sixty years. Even their makers will agree that they are fallible and quite insensitive. They may not even measure what they are supposed to measure. They are a beginning. We are improving.

But meanwhile, until such time as mechanical measuring devices become sensitive to all areas of human growth and development, we must continue our present course. This present course indicates, in essence, that we observe the child's own present behavior and performance in relation to his past behavior and performance to determine whether or not he has made progress in growth and development. Perhaps this, after all, is the best course.

THE KINDERGARTEN AND GROWTH

The kindergarten believes in growth. It helps to prepare the way, or set the stage, as it were, for growth to proceed. The kindergarten believes that a child, and all children, are capable of making strides toward desirable social and personal goals. These strides may be tiny steps for one child, giant steps for another, or medium-sized ones, depending on the child's own uniqueness and rate of growth. This rate of growth will differ and the level of achievement reached in a given time will also differ. But given an atmosphere which is encouraging, warm, and understanding, and a stimulating environment which lets him reach and stretch, and a child will grow in his own special way.

As an important phase in the educational continuum, the kindergarten carefully sets the stage for present success upon which later success can be built. This pays dividends for the child now and in the future.

What Else Does Kindergarten Do?

The kindergarten begins the all-important development of the basic attitudes which a child will have toward the educational program and toward school itself. If good attitudes are developed about school as a place to work and play, about teacher as a guide and help, about other children as friends, then this is a good beginning. And good beginnings are important. They are half the battle.

The kindergarten contributes toward the child's general adjustment. The social values he gains will come from guidance in group living and from the group climate. This climate, or atmosphere, is established by the interrelationships of the group to one another and to the teacher, and the teacher's relationships to individual children and to the whole group. There are many lessons to be gained from group living. Cooperation, responsibility, consideration, tolerance, respect for the rights of others are all important learnings.

The healthy development of the child's personality also is furthered by this experience and guidance in group living which goes on all during the kindergarten day. It is furthered, too, by the happy, cheerful atmosphere and by the program of satisfying activities which the kindergarten offers five-year-olds.

Whether the gains he makes in kindergarten in preparing for reading, writing, arithmetic place him ahead of other youngsters by the fifth or sixth grade of the elementary school is not clear from present studies. Whether the gains he makes in actually engaging in formal reading, writing, and arithmetic subject-matter place him ahead of other youngsters who do not receive this training in the very early years, also has not been satisfactorily proven. What has been shown from studies is that a good year in kindergarten in which the child has a broad program of activities, adequate materials and equipment, and satisfying relationships is a good foundation from which to carry on the later business of the elementary school. First-grade teachers also are in agreement that if a child has had this satisfying experience of a good year in kindergarten, his adjustment and progress in first grade are better. They feel that this kindergarten year makes a real contribution.

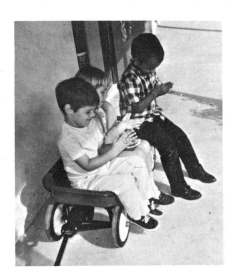

*Personality development and social adjustment are fur-
thered by experience and guidance in group living.*

A satisfying year for the child is important at any and every level. Growth and development are helped along by an accumulation of appropriate, satisfying, and stimulating experiences.

The value of the kindergarten program for the child in terms of his future success in the elementary school may be summed up as follows:

(a) The teamwork between home and school which is encouraged helps to make the child's transition to his beginning school experience an easier one.

(b) General adjustment to school is facilitated by the gradual transition between home and school stressed in the activities and focus of the kindergarten.

(c) A good year in kindergarten in which a broad program of activities is carried on, adequate materials and equipment are available, and satisfying relationships are experienced is a good foundation upon which to build later experience.

(d) The encouragement of the child's total development—physical, mental, social, and emotional—is an aid to his further growth and development.

(e) The readiness activities stressed are helpful in the child's transition to the more formal activities of the first-grade program, and the later grades of the school.

(f) The formation of favorable attitudes toward the educational program and school is encouraged, which pays off dividends in his feelings about school in the later grades.

(g) Personality development, and social adjustment are furthered by experiences and guidance in group living.

ROLE OF THE ELEMENTARY SCHOOL

The child's years in the elementary school should continue this upward and outward extension of his interests, appreciations, understandings, and skills begun in the kindergarten.

The elementary school should arrange an environment conducive to the physical development and health of the child.

The elementary school should encourage the social development of the child.

The elementary school should provide opportunities to promote the child's emotional development.

The elementary school should provide opportunities for the development of independent, creative thinking by the child.

The elementary school should provide opportunities for growth in the communicating arts, the fundamental skills and knowledges in order that the child may learn further and live more effectively.

The elementary school should provide opportunities for meeting the individual differences within each child.

The elementary school should encourage the development of understandings about the world of people and things.

The elementary school should foster the development of understanding and appreciation for the democratic way of life.

The elementary school should encourage the development of aesthetic appreciations in the child.

The elementary school should encourage the development of moral and spiritual values inherent in our culture.

The good elementary school is concerned with not only equipping a child with the basic skills needed in life situations, but also equipping him with understandings and knowledges needed to live more successfully with himself and with others in the world of today.

The emphasis in these roles is upon the total development of the child, which includes opportunities for his social, emotional mental, and physical growth.

The Kindergarten and the Elementary School

The kindergarten's roles are similar to those of the elementary school. The differences which exist between the kindergarten and the elementary school are not in the roles themselves, but in how these roles are fulfilled.

Both the kindergarten and the elementary school are concerned with this development of the whole child.

Both the kindergarten and the elementary school are concerned about promoting and maintaining the child's physical development and health.

The kindergarten program begins the important socialization process in giving a child the opportunity to further his contacts with other children and adults. The elementary school continues to encourage the child's social development.

The kindergarten program provides a rich environment for living, thinking, and learning. The elementary school, too, is concerned with providing opportunities for the development of independent, creative thinking by the child, and for meeting the individual differences in him and in the other children in his group.

The foundation for the three R's—reading, writing, and arithme-

tic—is cultivated in the kindergarten program. Also, the child is encouraged to expand language as a means of communication and
expression. The elementary school continues and enlarges upon this
foundation by providing opportunities for growth in the communicating arts and fundamental skills in order that the child may learn-
further and live more effectively.

A child's understanding of both the social world and the scientific
world is broadened in the kindergarten. The elementary school, too,
encourages the development of understanding about the world of
people and things.

The kindergarten program makes provision for satisfying aesthetic
experiences for the child. The elementary school, too, encourages the
development of aesthetic appreciations in the child.

The kindergarten program provides opportunities for the child to
develop his sense of responsibility. The elementary school includes
in its roles the encouragement of moral and spiritual values inherent
in our culture, and understanding and appreciation for the democratic
way of life.

DIFFERENCES

The kindergarten does not measure a child's achievement in
subjects such as arithmetic, social studies, science, reading, and the
other language arts. These learnings do go on, even though in a less
formal way, as befits the present development of the child. In addition, many other learnings take place, equally as important both at
this point in his life and for his later development.

While learning in the kindergarten encompasses the same general
subject-matter areas as are found in the elementary school as a whole,
the experiences a youngster will have within these areas necessarily
differ from those of older youngsters. The experiences differ because
of the nature, needs, and interests of the five-year-old. There is no set
body of facts and figures in which he must be drilled, which he must
memorize or be able to repeat. He is not seat-bound in the kindergarten. He is not paper-and-pencil-bound. He is not textbook-bound,
or workbook-bound, or test-bound.

He is experience-bent.

The kindergarten program is not a haphazard affair. It is not
dependent on whim or fancy. It is mapped out at the beginning of
the year. Even though a child's own interests will be considered,
whether they include baby hamsters or purple cows, he will also be
stimulated to form new interests. Even though the program is

flexible and subject matter is not mapped out as such, he will be exposed to and dip into a wide range of academic learnings. His planned experiences in kindergarten will contribute to his present development, as well as to the next step toward further learning. The lid is never on in the good kindergarten. The child is free to take the next step as he demonstrates that he is ready for it. There are signs. His teacher will be watching. If these signs indicate a go-ahead signal, he will delve ever more deeply into the learnings parents sometimes seem to feel he should be in a hurry to acquire.

Actually, a child has a long time to grow. He will be in school for more years than any other children in the history of our country, and perhaps of the world. We believe he can learn. We will do everything in our power to help him to learn.

But growth takes time. And worthwhile learning takes time. It includes time out for wonder, for interest, for satisfaction of old curiosities and stimulation of new curiosities. It includes time out for development of critical thinking, of intuitive thinking, and of analytical thinking.

This kind of thinking is not as likely to happen when a child is rooted to a chair and desk with stacks of books and workbooks to master, and sheets of paper to fill. This kind of thinking can happen when he has the freedom and time to move, to question, to probe, to use his five senses to the utmost, to experience fully. It can happen when he, in turn, is questioned and guided, and helped to discover for himself. It can happen when he is not overwhelmed by symbols of things before he is ready to leave the actual things themselves.

Focus

The focus is on *now*. How a child is now. What he is ready for now. What he can handle now. The concern is about now and about the future.

But this concern for the child's future is not in terms of expectancies which are demanding and set up artificial spurs to his present natural development. This concern for his future is in terms of providing him with experiences that fit him as he is now, and that will gradually lead him to further understandings, skills, appreciations, and interests in his ever-expanding world.

NOTES

[1]Reprinted from *Florida Education* by E. L. Widmer, by permission of Florida Education Association. Copyright 1966 by *Florida Education*.

Chapter 5

The Self-Concept

IMPORTANT PSYCHOLOGICAL DISCOVERY

The "Who am I," "Where am I," "How do I fit in," "What's important to me" evaluative questions which have plagued man for centuries are an integral part of the long process of growth as a human being. It is only man, *Homo sapiens,* who can truly influence his own destiny. Animals cannot do this. It is only man who can release the creative potential that is within him.

To do this, however, man must believe he can. For, this understanding of and belief in self acts as the facilitator which aids an individual in the achievement of his personal and social goals. A positive self-image, or self-concept, seems to be the "Open Sesame" to the attainment of the good life. The self-concept is unique to the development of the human species.

Maltz described this key to the good life.

> The most important psychologic discovery of this century is the discovery of the "self-image." Whether we realize it or not, each of us carries about with us a mental blueprint or picture of ourselves. It may be vague and ill defined to our conscious gaze. In fact, it may not be consciously recognizable at all. But it is there, complete down to the last detail. This self-image is our conception of the "sort of person I am." It has been built up from our own beliefs about ourselves. But most of these beliefs about ourselves have unconsciously been formed from our past experiences, our successes and failures, our humiliations, our triumphs, and the way other people have reacted to us, especially in early childhood. [1]

Development of the Self

The self is learned, then. It is developed out of the interaction between the individual and his environment, particulary the environment during the early years. Frank traced the earliest beginnings of the self concept during infancy:

75

When the baby is genuinely loved and given much needed warm reassuring mothering, with consideration for his helpless dependency and also his individuality, he begins to develop an image of the self, with feelings and expectations toward the world, that evokes his many capacities and latent potentialities. This prepares him for the experience of being transformed into a personality, the core of which is the image of the self that becomes symbolically expressed as I, me, my, and mine. The denial of benevolent practices and the experience of being verbally or physically punished, of feeling neglected or rejected, often leads to an image of the self that may seriously compromise his later learning experiences, especially his interpersonal relations and his ability to develop trust and confidence in the world which he has found so inhospitable.[2]

According to Combs and Snygg, the following ingredients are necessary for the development of an adequate personality: (1) a positive self-image, (2) an identification with others, (3) a rich and available perceptual field. They theorized that what an individual perceives in relation to self, becomes a part of his cognition of self in relation to others and the outside physical world.[3] His behavior is actually a reflection of his own perceptions of the kind of person he believes himself to be. Behavior, then, is determined by the individual's own perceptions of self at the instant of action.[4] Combs and Snygg detailed that the variables which affect an individual's perception are: (1) outside of the individual and are manipulative, (2) within the individual and indirectly manipulative as well as being inferred. Outside variables include time, opportunity, and the perceptual field. Variables within encompass the phenomenal self, the self-image, emotions and physiological processes.[5]

Since research tends to verify that this theory has some validity, we have at hand a valuable tool. Those of us who work for and with children can encourage the development of a positive self concept, promote coping tendencies and the growth of a healthy outlook on life. The failure syndrome which is demonstrated by children of all socioeconomic levels is an unnecessary waste of human resources. The vicious cycle inherent in failure experiences can be broken.

Erikson commented, "In order to create people who will function effectively . . . even the most 'savage' culture must strive for what we vaguely call a 'strong ego' . . . and above all to emerge from a long and unavoidably fearful infancy with a sense of identity and an idea of integrity."[6] Jahoda described the mentally healthy attitude toward the self in the following terms: "self-acceptance, self-confidence, or self-reliance . . . they express the judgment that in balance the self is 'good,' capable and strong."[7] In Combs view, positive experiences must be provided that can teach individuals they are positive people.[8]

Deutsch stressed success experience as the key to a positive view of self. Recent studies indicate that children are not only aware of their teachers' feelings about them, but tend to see themselves in the same light, and perform accordingly.[9] Combs pointed out, "it is people who see themselves as unliked, unwanted, unworthy, unimportant or unable who fill our jails, our mental hospitals, and our institutions."[10]

The following episode, recorded by the author in a kindergarten setting, reflects the wholesome relationships and positive attitudes toward self which this fine teacher stressed.

> There isn't one person today who forgot it was milk money day. I am very proud of you. An look who's back! Michael, we're very glad to see you. You've been like Mike Finnegan lately: in again and out again like Mike Finnegan's whiskers. Remember the story? "There was a man called Michael Finnegan. He grew whiskers on his chinnegan. The wind came out and blew them in agin. Poor old Michael Finnegan." So, don't get sick again. Stay with us. We have a lot of important things to do this week and need your help.

How early can this self-image be determined? The younger the child, the more expressions of self assertion may be apparent, but the less developed the self.[11] As the child grows in age as well as social experience, this self grows in depth and becomes less shallow; his own self-awareness expands with his deepening awareness of others.[12] How the child sees himself is perhaps the most important determiner of his behavior.

The listening, sensitive adult knows that children live in their own world as well as inhabit our spheres. Their own are infinitely more satisfying to them during the various stages of childhood development. It is when the adult world, a particular culture or social milieu, imposes its standards and enforces them early in a conditioning approach without recognition of and provision for the differences inherent within children, that trouble can arise.

Ilg and Ames summarized it thus:

> Let's consider for a minute the child we wish to know, on the threshhold of coming into the world on his own as a kindergartner. What a lovely image this word stimulates—a child's garden. Is it still the same garden it was or was meant to be? We need to ask

ourselves this question when we see the vultures of experimental
education poaching on this tender territory, forcing advanced
curricula in learning into the young child's receptive but unknowing mind. When and if this happens, the sympathetic flow between
adult and child may cease. . . .

What is worse, such an educator may be a slave to his own unknowing. He means well, but sometimes he can be misguided. He,
like the parent, needs to know more about development.[13]

Keeping in Touch

It is important to learn as much as is possible about this secret
world of childhood. However, it is more likely that sensitive insights
will be gained by the listening ear and understanding heart. These
insights can then reflect favorably on the kinds of environments provided for children. Unfortunately, there are many adults who have
lost touch with childhood, and display a general unfeeling amnesia
about the special needs of the young in our population. One wonders
if they were born old, or whether they passed through an early process
of conditioning which was especially rigorous, thorough and devas-
tatingly effective. Unfortunately, again, some of these adults are
working with children and conceive their role to be that of a lubricant
to speed children along the path of growth with little regard for the
differences, the life styles, the hopes, aspirations and fears of these
children.

Is it a waste of time for the teacher to try to discover more about
the young children in his group? No. This is not just interesting information to gain. It is vital to understand the child's view of life, his
evaluation of his world and his place in it. These are all important
factors in his growth and development, and later solid achievements.
When a child is given the feeling that he is a capable, worthwhile
human being, one who can learn and grow to be what he most desires
to be, he will be more likely to succeed. His actual performance on
learning tasks will be improved, as evidenced by research in this area.
"Factors such as expectancy for success or failure are apparently very
important in children's learning and problem solving, whether such
expectancies are the result of immediately prior experience in the
laboratory or an accumulation of past experiences from everyday
life."[14] Havighurst's theory of developmental tasks is worthy of note
here, since it offers more opportunities for the child to experience
success. And success breeds success. Havighurst stated that developmental tasks originate during periods of the growth sequence from

infancy through adolescence. The successful achievement of these tasks leads to the child's feelings of satisfaction and sense of achievement, while failure leads to disapproval by society, difficulty with later tasks and unhappiness in the child. Developmental tasks, according to Havighurst, arise from physical maturation, pressures from the cultural and social milieu into which the child is born, values, desires and personal goals emerging within the individual personality. Timing is all important. Utilization of the "teachable moment" is the critical factor in determining whether or not the child will learn.[15]

A Look at the Child

How can we discern when conditions are favorable for learning, when the teachable moments have arrived? The root of the answer to this question as well as to many other questions in education today lies at the heart of a thorough comprehension, comprehension of the individual's and group's patterns of growth and development.

How can the teacher find out about individual children in this early childhood group? How can he find out what is important to them, how these children see themselves? The first and still most helpful tool, with deepened understanding of the young child as the eventual goal, is observation of behavior. This observation should be in effect in a variety of unstructured as well as structured situations. It is not simply a look at the child. The orientation of this observation should be in terms of an honest appraisal of the child's actions, with one question always uppermost: How must he feel to behave in this manner? This is objective viewing with a large measure of empathy included.

Opportunities for Expression

Reflections of the world as they see it and their reactions to it are portrayed in children's forays into the various art media. Illuminating insights may be achieved through collections of a child's art products and his own interpretations of them. An outstanding teacher expressed it well:

> Children's art at its best is always something in the nature of a confession; it admits one instantly into the privacy of personal thinking and feeling. Most good art is confessional, I suspect; therefore it fails when it imitates or poses or attempts at concealment. The child knows that his world—the world of home and the world

of school—gives its praise to imitation and to posing-as-someone-other-than-self, and he discovers early that it is best to conceal.

Wherever creative work with children flourishes I seek the one who has opened up communication with them on the side of their secret unexpressed selves. She is usually a person who has no objections to anything that children tell her seriously; so she gets nearer and nearer to them, as one might become acquainted with birds; and as the communications develop into confessions she secures the astonishing results that are so often called gifts.[16]

A word of caution is in order. Teachers are not trained psychologists, and should not presume to judge a child's art work in relation to any suspected neurotic or psychotic tendencies. The individual teacher's role is to alert specialists to this possibility in the case of a child or children who are of special concern. In other words, to send out an SOS signal if a child exhibits possible symptoms of emotional disturbances is advisable, but not to attempt treatment. A visitor to a nursery school learned, to his chagrin, to withhold hasty judgment. He asked the head teacher, "Did you notice that little boy over there at the easel? He's using all dark colors in his painting. That could be serious, you know!"

The teacher replied, "Why don't you ask him why he chose those particular colors?"

The visitor, after asking the youngster about his selection of paints, received this terse explanation, "Cuz Susie's got all the other colors on her side."

And sure enough, Susie, the collector, had lined up all the paint jars on the other side of the double easel and was splashing a myriad of rainbow colors on her painting.

Dramatic play in the housekeeping center-of-interest as well as play activities in unstructured situations in general can be rich sources of understandings about young children. A group of four-year-olds were playing in the housekeeping corner of an early childhood room when the author arrived on a visit one morning. A sudden explosion of voices was heard and a loud, "Sybil, you get out of here! You can't play house with us!"

A sharp, "I don't care. I don't like you anyway," followed and a small figure stalked off, dragging a doll by the leg.

It did matter, very much, but she was not about to admit it. She moved to the piano and banged on the keys with one hand, holding onto the doll with the other.

Mary separated herself from the group in the housekeeping corner and walked over, determined to crush her enemy completely.

"We never want you to play with us again! Never!" Shift of gears now, to, "What are you doing?"

"I'm playing the piano," Then, remembering afresh, "I don't want to play with you."

Mary, deciding her job of demolishing hadn't been thorough enough, continued, "You can't come to my party." Logic makes a tentative appearance at about the age of three years, but has a long developmental period, as illustrated by four-year-old Mary's final blow, "I won't even tell you when my birthday is!"

"I don't care."

A quick shift of the emotions occurred when Mary, also engaged in trying out the keys of the old piano, pushed down on one that did not respond.

"Look, Sybil. I pushed this key down, but there's no noise."

"Yeah. It doesn't work." Giggles, as they both tried to no avail.

When the author left shortly afterwards, she glanced back at the piano. Two heads were still bent over the keys. All undying enmity was forgotten.

This episode highlights social and emotional levels of development as well as the reason distraction is considered an effective technique by early childhood educators. The quick shifts of interest and attention which are generally in evidence during these early years can be used to advantage by the teacher who wishes to prevent or cope with troubles brewing in a conflict situation.

Talking it out, and discussions in general can be other helpful techniques in finding out how a child sees himself. A group of disadvantaged Negro youngsters in a kindergarten were talking about their goal aspirations in an informal discussion group one day. There were colorful pictures around the room of men and women engaged in various occupations.

"I'm gonna be a fireman," stated one.

"Not me," asserted another youngster. "I'm gonna be a doctor or a nurse."

"Me, I'm gonna bake bread."

When their ideas had been freely expressed their teacher realized that one quiet lad had not taken part in the lively exchange.

"And what do you want to be when you grow up?" she asked the dark-skinned boy.

"I want to be a Puerto Rican," replied the child instantly.

A commentary, indeed, on young children's view of the adult world and its hierarchy of values.

The following responses were recorded by a teacher of an all Negro class of six-year-olds:

Teacher: Do you see any Negroes in this room?
Child: No.
Teacher: What are you?
Child: A girl.
Teacher: Are you a Negro?
Second child: Yes.
Teacher: Is Brenda a Negro?
Child: No.
Teacher: Who are Negroes?
Child: Boys are Negroes.
Teacher: Are you a Negro?
Child: Yes.
Teacher: Is your mother a Negro?
Fourth child: Yes.
Teacher: Is your daddy a Negro?
Child: Yes.
Teacher: Are you a Negro?
Child: Yes.
Teacher: Is Sandra a Negro?
Sixth child: No.
Teacher: Are you a Negro?
Child: No.
Teacher: Who are you?
Child: The princess.
Teacher: Are you a Negro?
Seventh child: No (light-skinned male).
Teacher: Is your mother a Negro?
Eighth child: Yes.
Teacher: Is your sister a Negro?
Child: No.
Teacher: Is your daddy a Negro?
Child: Yes.
Teacher: What are you?
Child: A boy.
Teacher: Well, who is a Negro?
Ninth child: My mother and my daddy.
Teacher: Why?
Child: Because they are grown.

Puppetry is another fertile means of encouraging expression in the early years, and affording the listening adult a precious glimpse into the child's world. A puppet can say anything because, after all, who would spank a puppet? This seems to be the feeling of children who use puppets in a variety of forms. Puppets are also excellent language facilitators.

A kindergarten teacher reported that she was worried about a boy in her group who never opened his mouth to say a single word during the entire first six weeks of school. She was seriously considering a special request for school psychological services. One day she brought in some paper-bag puppets to demonstrate to the youngsters the variety of approaches possible in a puppet-making project underway. "When that boy caught sight of the paper bags, he made a bee-line for them, grabbed one, put it over his head and started talking a blue streak. I was so amazed, my mouth dropped open. Here I had been trying for six weeks to get him to say something and a glorified paper bag did it! He hasn't stopped talking since."

The use of three wishes is another useful device to encourage self-expression and also provide fruitful insights. "Happiness is . . ." and "sadness is . . ." are other extensions of projective techniques which have been employed in some early childhood settings with interesting results. Unless the meanings of happiness and sadness are understood by the youngsters, however, they will be mere symbolic abstractions. Five- and six-year-olds who were asked about happiness and its special meaning for them, had a variety of replies:

"Happiness is a nice place to live."
"When you love each other. When my mother loves me."
"When my mother buys me new shoes."
"Happiness is five dollars."
"Having a birthday."
"Playing with children."
"Thanksgiving."
"Happiness is listening to music."
"Happiness is five girls." (This from a girl with five sisters!)
"Having a friend."
"Happiness is visiting grandma and eating there."

Summary

These are some of the tools and techniques which have been found useful in arriving at a better understanding of young children and their development. Armed with this understanding, teachers can promote effective learning experiences and combat the poor self-concept which some children display, as well as encourage the development of a picture of the self which is a positive one. The fundamental step in helping a child to feel worthwhile, however, is to believe in the intrinsic worth of all children, to believe they can grow as basic human beings. Believing in children is a powerful medicine which can work wonders. Our optimism and consistent positive actions within a supportive environment will be reflected in children's performance.

"Although," delineated Hawk, "education is not and should not be perceived as psychotherapy, the educational process, by its very nature, affects a reconstruction of the self-concepts of children."[17] Let us not perpetuate a feeling of failure, of worthlessness, in any child with whom we come in contact. The key to successful achievement and personal satisfaction is found in the wholesome, positive, personal relationships and interrelationships established in the early childhood classrooms. It is every child's birthright to have adults who believe in him.

LEARNING

The Search for Evidence

A passage from *Alice in Wonderland* between Alice and the Cheshire Cat bears repeating in view of recommendations by some professionals today who propose to throw out everything not proven empirically or testable by means of paper and pencil measurements. Alice asks

"Would you tell me please, which way I ought to go from here?"

"That depends a good deal on where you want to get to," said the Cat.

"I don't much care where—" said Alice.

"Then it doesn't matter which way you go," said the Cat.

"—so long as I get *somewhere*," Alice added as an explanation.

"Oh, you're sure to do that," said the Cat, "if you only walk long enough."[18]

In the meantime, while we "walk long enough" searching for empirical evidence and behavioral objectives, we may overlook the live bodies of young children in our early childhood settings who need guidance in stimulating environments right now.

Many years ago education was believed to consist of a predetermined set body of facts. The student's role was that of a passive receptacle, much like an empty glass. The teacher's role was that of a filled pitcher. He poured facts into the empty glass, or student. The success or failure of this pouring-in process known as education was determined by the amount and accuracy of the facts which the student could regurgitate on cue in a testing situation. To survive this process known as education, one had to be hardy, to be able to "take it," both physically and mentally. The mind was thought to need stretching and exercising on materials both abundant and difficult, much as a muscle needs exercise. Needless to say, this was education for the few. These few were not necessarily the most able. They were the toughest and hardiest. The many stopped.

In reviewing our current plight, this is the picture which emerges: We are not advanced in our own knowledge and skills in the area of tests and measurements. We do not know enough about cognitive development or the affective domain, or any other domain. We do not know exactly how to match the materials of learning with the child's developmental level. We are in no position to prepare careful blueprints which will maximize a child's growth and development by means of the environments we provide and with which he interacts. We simply do not know enough, and frankly, cannot wait while we "walk long enough" to find out. The children are here now. The acid test at this stage of our knowing and skills, or lack of knowing and lack of skills should be in the form of a very practical question. Does it work with young children? Or, better still, the question should be refocused to: Does it work with this particular child and group of young children? How is he reacting? How are they reacting? Is it of short duration, a one-shot approach? Or do they seem to be carrying it over to other situations, transferring it? This "it" may be in the realm of problem-solving techniques, methodology, curriculum, materials, ways of dealing with the dynamics of group structure, a discovery approach, or perhaps, a useful technique to encourage the development of auditory discrimination.

Learning is not the mysterious process that we make of it. With a generous serving of common sense laced with actual experience with young children in early childhood settings plus some suggested guidelines already available from research on learning, we can provide stimulating climates for growth and learning right now. To those who must have instant proof in the form of statistical analysis, we offer this reply:

sensitive observation of an individual child by a knowledgeable, experienced, understanding teacher is still the best index of a child's
progress. Given our present dilemma of frank ignorance and blunt
tools, statistical groupings are not the panacea toward progress in
understanding children that some individuals and groups assert. We
are still in the dark ages, generally speaking, when we insist on research proof from sterile, laboratory settings and then institute attempts to force these findings into classroom contexts. We are dis-
trustful of our own considerable wisdom slowly built up from practical
experience with children within and outside of educational settings.
We are hesitant about protesting against practices which may force
mental growth, but to the neglect and, perhaps, at the expense of the
rest of the child. In the process, the field of education is losing creative,
intelligent, child-centered professionals and potential professionals
who are, after all, the real answer to any lasting progress we may
achieve in early childhood.

The Process Itself

We can stress this about learning: for learning to make an impression, it must have meaning for a particular learner in terms of
his past experience and understandings, as well as present interests
and needs. The future is still too nebulous for it to have any real at-
traction or magnetic pull toward a better life for the young learner.
That comes later, much later. For learning to make an impression,
the focus must be on the learner and what he brings to the situation.

> Of all the forces operating in a school the energy of the learner
> is the greatest. If it is "turned on" at full voltage—and directed
> straight into the task at hand—it is almost irresistible. Even if
> teaching is mediocre and material resources are meager, the young-
> ster will somehow move ahead. But if it is "turned off"—or diverted
> from the task or opposed to it—nothing else matters very much.
>   That flow of energy is controlled by the learner's perceptions.
> . . . If a full charge of energy is to be delivered to any learning task,
> two conditions must prevail: the learner must see the task with clear
> eyes and sense that it is relevant to his private goals; and he must
> have faith that he is ready to tackle it, that he is the kind of person
> who ought to do this sort of thing and who can do it if he stretches.[19]

If this, then, has been a learning situation invested with real
meanings for the learner, the learning itself becomes incorporated into
his "schemata." It becomes a part of him. The process is helped
along by having a wealth of direct experience and a multisensory

approach to the environment with much manipulation during discovery and problem-solving situations.

Terrell hypothesized the potency of the manipulative process. He found the manipulative process an aid in learning: " . . . Children learned better to generalize the concept of large when they played a game of pretending to put promised candy in a bag, as compared with a mere promise of candy or with only a flashing light to signal the correct response."[20] Jensen noted that mere visual experience of objects accompanied by verbalization was not sufficient. Children who were merely shown objects which were then named did not learn as much or as rapidly as the children who were given the objects to handle at the same time that they were named.[21]

This regard for the learner as a total reacting unit, a whole organism, represents progress. It was not always so, and unfortunately, there are current signs that we may be regressing again in the zeal displayed by some to force difficult subject matter down into the lower grades, as well as "cover" more subject areas focusing on abstract materials.

Children of all levels in our schools frequently find it difficult to see any real connection between what happens in school and what happens outside of school. And unless we do a selling job on the actual relationship which can and does exist between what is learned in our school context and its relevance to children's concerns in doing, thinking and feeling, we have lost the real battle. The bodies are there in the seats as a captive audience, but these, too, frequently leave as soon as they are legally permitted to do so. Lee stated:

> Experience has proved that children with a wide range of concerns, competencies, and enthusiasms and with widely differing self-concepts, learning styles, goals, and purposes do not learn the same thing at the same time in the same way. This principle is generally accepted but not widely practiced. Failure to do so is rationalized by the amount of material to be covered and the number of children in a class.[22]

The concern for what is important for children must translate itself into practical realities which never lose sight of the young learner in an overplaced zeal to stuff him with the staggering amount of material in our curricula today. There is a complex interrelationship at work in a performance by a learner. His actual cognitive level of development, motivational and emotional factors, plus the achievements of this child are the components inextricably involved in his every performance. "Covering" a subject generally refers to memorization of printed and verbalized material involving symbol recognition. Learning and thinking may have nothing to do with this exercise in mental gymnastics.

Time and patience are indispensable requirements for the development of potential. We should remember: "to cover" is no guarantee that "to learn" has occurred.

How intent are we upon "covering" the subject matter? A teacher of a first-grade class commented to the author recently, in describing a typical day's program, that she still provided for one fifteen minute recess period a day. She said it apologetically, and hastened to add, "we're getting rid of that soon. There just isn't time enough for everything." No there is not time enough for everything. But let us be certain we are not throwing out the baby with the bath water. The children in that class had not even had any oasis of kindergarten experience to remember, since kindergartens are not as yet an integral part of the public schools in that state. Life, indeed, has become a grim struggle to keep up from the first day of school. Small wonder that reports from pediatricians are beginning to form an illuminating pattern. It seems that an increasing number of their young patients exhibit disturbing symptoms which correlate with the beginning of regular school attendance. The symptoms include upset stomachs, vomiting, lassitude, and the general "miseries." It is becoming the rule rather than the exception to crush a tranquilizer in the child's breakfast juice in order to facilitate the going-to-school process.

Tragic, indeed, when one reflects upon Spodek's statement:

> What I have been trying to suggest is that the question of motivation, or at least of having teachers develop motivational devices for use in early childhood classes, is not a productive one. Young children can learn. Young children want to learn. Young children need little incitement to learn when the modes of learning provided to them are consistent with their own wishes for exploration and their own needs for movement, and when the activities that are designed for them by the teacher are tailored to their needs, their behavior patterns, and their developmental levels. The teacher of young children could benefit more by looking for new and exciting ways of conducting classes and introducing knowledge than by devising cute ways of moving or inciting children to function in dull, inappropriate classroom activities.[23]

Needs

Young children need love, a sense of security and trust in their world. They need people concerned enough about them to carefully

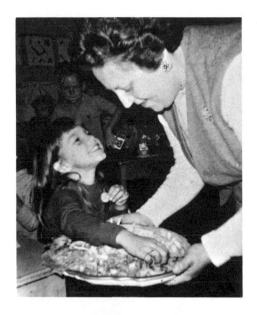

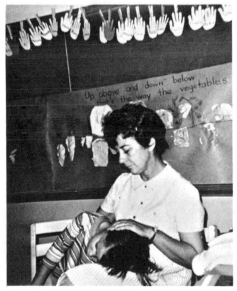

An encouraging, supportive atmosphere.

make plans for and with them. But not rigid plans which lose sight of them as individuals, or which do not reflect respect for them as individuals. The lesson to be learned is that we must become more aware in our programs for young children of the children themselves. They need many opportunities to react within an environment geared to their individual differences, to choose selectively, to respond and interact within an enriched environment concerned with them and their actual current and expanding interests and capabilities. And we must free them as individuals to do this. If we deem it important to encourage and aid our young children in their process of becoming and achieving, then we must work within the realities of individual growth and development, and design accordingly.

Learning-Becoming

What should be at the core of the learning-becoming process? Based upon our present stage of knowledge in this latter half of the twentieth century, the following list encompasses areas worthy of reflection and implementation during the critical years of early childhood:

1. Concern for and understanding of the child as an individual as well as a member of groups.
2. Recognition of the value of the group and the group climate in the child's social and cognitive growth.
3. Realization and implementation of the fact that the young child's modes of thinking and learning styles are different from those of adults.
4. Respect for readiness factors which determine the teachable moment.
5. Comprehension of the critical nature of concept formation for the child's future intellectual growth.
6. Profound respect for the value of play in the young child's growth and development.
7. Concern and provision for the special health and physical needs of this period.
8. Cognizance of the importance of a positive self-concept for optimal development.

SUGGESTED READINGS

Association for Childhood Education International. *Basic Human Values for Childhood Education*. Washington, D.C.: The Association, 1962.

———. *Feelings and Learning*. Washington, D.C.: The Association, 1965.

———. *Implications of Basic Human Values for Education*. Washington, D.C.: The Association, 1964.

———. *Toward Better Kindergartens*. Washington, D.C.: The Association, 1966.

Benedict, Ruth. *Patterns of Culture*. Boston: Houghton Mifflin, 1934.

Bettelheim, Bruno. *Dialogues with Mothers*. New York: Free Press, 1962.

Bruner, Jerome S. *Toward a Theory of Instruction*. New York: W. W. Norton and Company, Inc., 1966.

California State Department of Education. *A Teacher's Guide to Education in Early Childhood*. Sacramento: The Department, 1956.

Chauncey, Henry (ed.). *Soviet Preschool Education*. Princeton, N. J.: Educational Testing Service, 1969.

Christianson, Helen, Mary M. Rogers, and Blanche A. Ludlum. *The Nursery School: Adventure in Living and Learning*. Boston: Houghton Mifflin Company, 1961.

Cole, Luella. *History of Education From Socrates to Montessori*. New York: Rinehart and Company, 1950.

Combs, Arthur W., and Donald Snygg. *Individual Behavior, A Perceptual Approach to Behavior*. Rev. ed. New York: Harper and Row, Publishers, 1959.

Comenius, John Amos. *The School of Infancy*. Edited by Ernest M. Eller. Chapel Hill: University of North Carolina Press, 1956.

Council of Chief State School Officers. *Responsibilities of State Departments of Education for Nursery Schools and Kindergartens*. Washington, D.C.: The Council, 1961.

Crosby, Muriel. *Curriculum Development in a Changing Society*. Boston: D. C. Heath and Company, 1964.

Cutts, N. E., and N. Mosley. *Providing for Individual Differences in the Elementary School*. Englewood Cliffs, N.J.: Prentice-Hall, Inc., 1960.

Department of Elementary School Principals. *Those First School Years*. Washington, D.C.: The Department, National Education Association, 1960.

Dinkmeyer, Don, and Rudolf Dreikurs. *Encouraging Children to Learn: The Encouragement Process*. Englewood Cliffs: N.J., 1963.

Educational Policies Commission and American Association of School Administrators. *Universal Opportunity for Early Childhood Education*. Washington, D.C.: National Education Association, 1964.

Featherstone, Joseph. *What's Happening in British Classrooms*. Washington, D. C.: The New Republic, 1244 19th Street, N.W.

Forest, Ilse. *Preschool Education: A Historical and Critical Study*. New York: Macmillan Company, 1927.

Foshay, Arthur W., and Kenneth D. Wann. *Children's Social Values*. New York: Columbia University Press, 1954.

Friedenberg, E. Z. *Coming of Age in America: Growth and Acquiescence*. New York: Random House, Inc., 1963.

Frost, Joel (ed.). *Early Childhood Education Rediscovered, Readings*. New York: Holt, Rinehart and Winston, Inc., 1968.

Ginzberg, E. (ed.). *The Nation's Children, Volume 1, The Family and Social Change*. New York: Columbia University Press, 1960.

_____. *The Nation's Children, Volume 3, Problems and Prospects*. New York: Columbia University Press, 1960.

Headley, Neith. *The Kindergarten: Its Place in the Program of Education*. New York: Center for Applied Research in Education, Inc., 1965.

Hechinger, Fred M. (ed.). *Pre-School Education Today*. Garden City, New York: Doubleday and Company, 1966.

Hymes, James L., Jr. *Teaching the Child Under Six*. Columbus, Ohio: Charles E. Merrill Publishing Company, 1968.

Kearney, Nolan C. *Elementary School Objectives*. A Report Prepared for the Mid-Century Committee on Outcomes in Elementary Education. New York: Russell Sage Foundation, Inc., 1953.

Kessen, William, and George Mandler (eds.). *The Child*. New York: John Wiley and Sons, Inc., 1965.

Mead, Margaret, and M. Wolfenstein (eds.). *Childhood in Contemporary Cultures*. Chicago: University of Chicago Press, 1955.

Mitchell, Lucy Sprague. *Our Children and Our Schools*. New York: Simon and Schuster, 1950.

Monroe, W. S. (ed.). *Comenius' School of Infancy*. Boston: D.C. Heath and Company, 1908.

Montagu, Ashley. *Education and Human Relations.* New York: Grove Press, Inc., 1958.

Montessori, Maria. *The Montessori Method.* New York: Frederick A. Stokes Company, 1912.

———. *The Discovery of the Child.* Madras, India: Kalaskshetra Publications; sold by The Theosophical Press, Wheaton, Ill. 1962.

National Education Association. ASCD. *Leadership for Improving Instruction.* Association for Supervision and Curriculum Department Yearbook. Washington, D.C.: 1960.

National Education Association. Department of Elementary-Kindergarten-Nursery Education. *Kindergarten Education.* Washington, D.C.: The Association, 1968.

———. *Kindergarten Today.* Washington, D.C.: The Association, 1963.

———. *The Evaluation of Teaching.* Washington, D.C.: The Association, 1966.

———. *The Step Beyond:* Creativity. Washington, D.C.: The Association, 1964.

National Society for the Study of Education. *Early Childhood Education.* 46th Yearbook. Chicago: University of Chicago Press, 1947.

Passow, A. Harvey (ed.). *Curriculum Crossroads.* New York: Columbia University Press, 1962.

Rasmussen, Margaret (ed.). *Don't Push Me!* Washington, D.C.: Association for Childhood Education International, 1960.

Sears, R. R. et al. *Patterns of Child Rearing.* Evanston, Ill. Row, Peterson and Company, 1957.

Trager, Helen, and Marian Yarrow. *They Learn What They Live.* New York: Harper and Brothers, 1952.

United States Office of Education. *Educating Children in Nursery School and Kindergarten.* Washington, D.C.: U.S. Government Printing Office, 1964.

Vandewalker, Nina C. *The Kindergarten in American Education.* New York: The Macmillan Company, 1913.

Wilds, Elmer Harrison. *The Foundations of Modern Education.* New York: Farrar and Rinehart, Inc., 1936.

Yeomans, Edward. *Education for Initiative & Responsibility.* Boston, Massachusetts: National Association of Independent Schools.

Zirbes, Laura. *Focus on Values in Elementary Education.* New York: G. P. Putnam's Sons, 1960.

NOTES

[1]Maxwell Maltz, *Psycho-Cybernetics* (Englewood Cliffs, N. J.: Prentice-Hall, 1965), p. 2.

[2]Lawrence K. Frank, *On the Importance of Infancy* (New York: Random House, Inc., 1966), pp. 148–149.

[3]Arthur W. Combs and Donald Snygg, *Individual Behavior* (New York: Harper & Row, Publishers, 1949), pp. 237–265.

[4]*Ibid.*, p. 240.

[5]*Ibid.*, p. 260.

[6]Erik H. Erikson, *Childhood and Society* (New York: W. W. Norton and Company, Inc., 1950), p. 160.

[7]Marie Jahoda, *Current Concepts of Positive Mental Health* (New York: Basic Books, Inc., 1959), p. 24.

[8]Arthur W. Combs (ed.), *Perceiving, Behaving, Becoming* (Washington, D.C.: Association for Supervision and Curriculum Development, 1962).

[9]Martin Deutsch, "The Disadvantaged Child and the Learning Process," in A. H. Passow (ed.), *Education in Depressed Areas* (New York: Columbia University Press, 1965).

[10]*Combs, op. cit.*, p. 52.

[11]Arnold Gesell and Frances L. Ilg, *The Child From Five to Ten* (New York: Harper and Brothers, 1946), p. 317.

[12]*Ibid.*, p. 317.

[13]Frances L. Ilg and Louise Ames, *School Readiness* (New York: Harper and Row, 1965), pp. 32–33.

[14]Morton W. Weir, "Children's Behavior in Probabilistic Tasks," in Willard W. Hartup and Nancy L. Smothergill (eds.), *The Young Child* (Washington, D.C.: National Association for Education of Young Children, 1967), p. 153.

[15]Robert J. Havighurst, *Human Development and Education* (New York: Longmans, Green and Company, 1953), pp. 1–5.

[16]Hughes Mearnes, *Creative Power: The Education of Youth in the Creative Arts*. 2nd rev. ed. (New York: Dover Publications, Inc., 1958), p. 80.

[17]Travis L. Hawk, "Self Concepts of the Socially Disadvantaged," *The Elementary School Journal*, Vol. 67 (January 1967), p. 197.

[18]Lewis Carroll, *Alice's Adventures in Wonderland.*

[19]Fred T. Wilhelms and Paul B. Diederich, "The Fruits of Freedom," in Fred Wilhelms (ed.), *Evaluation as Feedback and Guide* (Washington, D.C.: Association for Supervision and Curriculum Development, 1967), pp. 234–235.

[20]Symposium, "Learning and Cognition and Intelligence," *Child Development*, No. 31, 1960, p. 237.

[21]Arthur R. Jensen, "Learning in the Preschool Years," in Williard W. Hartup and Nancy Smothergill (eds.), *The Young Child, op. cit.*, p. 131.

[22]Doris M. Lee, *Diagnostic Teaching* (Washington, D.C.: National Education Association, 1966), p. 6.

[23]Bernard Spodek, "Motivation in Early Education," in *Motivation* (Washington, D.C.: National Education Association, 1968), pp. 12–13.

Part III

Design for the Early Years

Chapter 6

The Young Learner

It is a curious fact that throughout the history of education most of the reforms and modifications in educational procedure have come first in the training of young children. These have been followed by modifications in the lower grades; later the procedures are extended into the upper grades, then into the high school, and ultimately into the college. It is possible that young children with their freshness, spontaneity and curiosity constantly put our formalized and traditional activities to the test, and that, because they never seem to fit the educational pattern which we set for them, the continual changes which later modify our formal procedures are set in motion.[1]

A HUMBLE PROP

The author, on an inspection tour of early childhood programs in a northern metropolitan area, became both an observer and a participant in the conversation period of a kindergarten class one crisp autumn day. Kenny, who had volunteered to share an experience with the listening group of fives, sturdily stood up next to his teacher, gazed down at the children and then promptly forgot what he wanted to say.

"Did you have something to show us?" inquired his teacher gently.

"Oh yeah!" relieved, he dug into his pocket and fished out a brown nut. "I found this on the way to school," he said, holding it up for all to inspect.

He was just about to sit down, when his teacher, an experienced, successful guide for these young learners, asked, "Tell us. What kind of a nut is it?"

He didn't know, nor did any of the other children. Neither, it seemed, did the teacher know. "How about the visitor in the back of the room?" They turned to the author in her quiet corner. Unfortunately, no help from that quarter either.

What to do?

"Well children, how are we going to find out what kind of a nut this is?"

Here was a very real problem. Solutions were proposed, and each in turn given a hearing and carefully considered.

"We could plant it," offered Juan.

"Yes," the teacher agreed. "Do you remember, though, how long it took for our sweet potato plant to start growing?" she appealed to Juan and the other children. They decided the answer might take weeks to develop, much too long to wait.

"Eat it," suggested a chubby little girl.

"Do you always know the exact name of what you are eating? Sometimes, do you just like the taste, or decide you don't want any more because it's bitter or sour?"

They all nodded thoughtfully.

Then it came. The answer that could serve as a useful tool for now and in the future.

"Look it up in a nut book!" submitted Mike.

An important learning experience with problem solving at its base. No expensive equipment required, just a simple prop. Plus a creative teacher who capitalized upon the learnings to be gained from this prop and the judicious use of questions to prime the children's thinking. They decided to investigate the place where "nut books" could be found. As it turned out, this involved a group trip to the local library and the beginnings of a nodding acquaintanceship with the reference section.

RAW MATERIALS

In considering optimal programs for young children, we must be aware of the built-in, natural resources they bring within their small personages. They are not content with merely asking about the hows, and whys and wherefores. They investigate, probe, experiment and test with all the awesome energy of their young, active bodies. When a program is well designed, it recognizes and incorporates these children's great interest in and urge to discover more about the physical and social world surrounding them. A well-designed program recognizes and utilizes these allies of learning: interest, curiosity, activity.

This activity is special. It incorporates personal involvement of a kind which plunges youngsters into a range of direct and vicarious experiences. These experiences serve as a backdrop for concept formation.

Young children's play activities can infuse learning with the zest and purpose. The value of a "gamelike" context with "inductive teaching or the discovery method" as the approach is discussed in Wallach and Kogan.[2] This approach which young children take to readily and easily, fosters both creativity and intelligence. "If teachers can be taught to deemphasize the success-failure aspects of the learning process and to encourage children to approach school assignments in a spirit of associative play, much will have been gained."[3]

The consuming curiosity which is an integral expression of a healthy young child's urge to find out, is another ally of the learning process. It needs careful nourishment in a warm supportive environment, however, if it is to remain undiminished. This questing for answers can be uncomfortable for busy adults to live with at times. One youngster who arrived at a Head Start center was convinced his name was Shut Up, for obvious reasons. The time to become concerned is when the questions stop.

Good questions relate to something in the child's immediate experience and send him in search of information. Poor questions allow only for a correct-incorrect, recall approach and lead the child nowhere else beyond the initial question. The wise adult will utilize questions to cue a youngster in on possible solutions to a problem situation, realizing it is what this youngster discovers himself that has most meaning for him. "It doesn't work? I wonder why? Let's take a look. Do you suppose it might have anything to do with that back wheel?" "John won't let you set next to him at the table? Well, how could you make him feel friendly towards you? We usually like to sit next to our friends." "You're right. Our barometer isn't working properly. Have we changed anything or done anything to make it react in that way?" "How do you think you could settle this argument over the tricycle so that you both feel right about it?"

We must create situations which not only permit questioning but encourage and utilize it. Questions are tokens of the young child's curiosity and important resources which can help to prime his thinking.

The raw materials which the early childhood youngster brings with him, his interest, curiosity and activity, are actually allies of the learning process. A program is successful to the extent that it utilizes these children's own very real efforts to learn about and understand the immediate environment which surrounds and affects them.

If these youngsters are not actively interested, or curious, or questioning, look to:

1. The teacher: his knowledge and understanding of children in general and a current group in particular, plus his expectancies for individuals within the group.
2. The children: possible background factors contributing to problems in physical, social, emotional and intellectual growth areas.
3. The program and curriculum: its demands and expectations.
4. The teacher: his grasp of program, curriculum and teaching practices in relation to this group of children.
5. The materials and equipment: their intrinsic appeal or lack of appeal for the children.

VALUE OF THE GROUP

The conception of the educational enterprise as a vehicle for bringing enlightenment to groups of "have-nots," or learners, by means of leadership by the adult "haves," or teachers, is an obstacle to innovation. So, too, is our futile attempt to gather the "have-nots" together into homogeneous groups.

Children can help one another to learn, if given the opportunity. Exchanges between these "have-nots" can be fruitful and a decided boost for the learning process.

The ability of children to help one another to learn has not been adequately plumbed, and certainly not exploited as a valuable resource. The value of the group as a many-faceted vehicle for change and for the growth of its individual members, rather than just a convenient collection of bodies, has been neglected since our colonial start as a nation. Then, for a time, expediency forced us into the venerable one-room schoolhouse in which various chronological ages were represented in the children gathered together from the surrounding countryside. It was common practice for the children to help one another while teacher was working on the development of special skills with a small group gathered around his desk. There was no clear-cut dividing line between the haves and the have-nots then, perhaps because there was need for many helping hands within such a wide range of individual differences.

These one-room schoolhouses were the first examples of the organizational pattern known today as multiage grouping. This approach offers a rich variety of situations which are conducive to flourishing interrelationships among children of different developmental levels and chronological ages.

Individual differences are still with us and will always remain. They should not be considered inconvenient obstacles. It is time for us to stop our pursuit of an impossible and foolish ideal: the homogeneous group. It is time to face the fact that individual differences are here to stay. No process of selection can ever lump abilities into categories labeled as superior, average, and below average in all areas, or even within the same area. A homogeneous group does not and cannot exist. Differences are resources which should be exploited to the hilt by the educational establishment. The actual encouragement and development of diverse styles in our learners is possible through opportunities for free interchange among various age and developmental levels at work in a variety of experiences that are grounded in manipulative activities.

Such settings are more frequently found in British infant schools than in schools for the early childhood and primary grade youngsters in the United States. In describing the best of the British infant schools, the following points are worthy of note:

> . . . Here the child's experience is integrated, more continuous, more of a piece. There is no dividing line between work and play; and indeed for a five-year-old it is hard to distinguish between playing with a balance and working on weight and measurement problems.
> The children's response to this freedom was reflected in the atmosphere of the classroom; a busy, constructive environment. The classrooms were filled with a busy hum—not silence, but not noise either. Children talked to each other about what they were doing. I watched two seven-year-old girls telling each other long involved stories about the building they had built together. When the teacher was occupied, children would ask other children for help in reading or spelling. This constructive interaction was particularly marked in schools that practiced vertical grouping, placing children of different ages in the same class. Here the older children took responsibility for the younger children. Since they were all at different stages of physical development it seemed natural to the children that they should be at different academic levels. The children felt free to ask and to give assistance among themselves.[4]

Piaget's emphasis on social interaction can be directly infused into the curriculum by means of the following suggestions: "For example, small groups of children might be assigned to work together,

*Individual and Group Activities in the Work-Play
Period.*

not, as is so often the case, merely carrying on parallel activities, but actually sharing them. Children who seem to have understood a particular concept might be given opportunities to help children who appear less certain."[5]

Children can help one another to important emotional, social, motor and cognitive learnings. It is high time to include them as largely untapped resources of great value to our educational enterprises.

THAT GLOW OF ACHIEVEMENT

Nothing breeds success as well as success itself. The "I can do it," "I did it!" perceptions are critical ones for further growth and development. These perceptions leave lasting impressions which can affect future performance.

How can we help young children to feel this sense of mastery? First, teacher expectation influences a child's performance. Consistent actions which demonstrate, "I know you can do it!" will spur a child on to new heights. Rosenthal's study on the influence of teacher's expectations on children's performance has shown that a child will do as well or as badly in school as his teacher thinks he will.[6] The performance level of groups of youngsters of normal ability whose teachers were told that they were rated in the high ability range increased significantly. And conversely, those actually in the high ability range who were labeled as slower learners for the purpose of the study did not show a comparable growth in achievement.

Next, the focus should be on what the young child is able to do. We start where he is, and go on from there. This necessitates arranging and manipulating the environment to insure accomplishment. Many opportunities for "quickie successes" help children to gain the feelings of achievement so necessary to their launching into more difficult tasks. A steady procession of unrelieved failure experiences in which the job was simply too demanding, too uninteresting, too incomprehensible is damaging and a waste of time for all concerned. It is small wonder that these are the children who swell the ranks of the dropout, or, more aptly, the pushout.

Any teacher worthy of the title must arrange the environment so that each child has a feeling of accomplishment, however small the completed task may be in adult eyes. Any child who feels he is a failure, who "can't do anything right," is the teacher's failure. Nothing breeds success as well as success itself.

NOTES

[1]John E. Anderson, "Changing Emphases in Early Childhood Education," *School Society*, No. 49 (1939), p. 1.

[2]Michael A. Wallach and Nathan Kogan, *Modes of Thinking in Young Children* (New York: Holt, Rinehart and Winston, Inc., 1965), p. 323.

[3]*Ibid.*, p. 323.

[4]Joy Schlesinger, *Leicestershire Report: The Classroom Environment*, unpublished mimeo, Fall 1966, p. 3.

[5]Millie Almy, with Edward Chittenden and Paula Miller, *Young Children's Thinking* (New York: Columbia University Press, 1966), p. 138.

[6]"Teacher's Expectation Affects Pupil's Efforts," *Today's Child*, October 1967, p. 8.

Chapter **7**

In Kindergarten¹

Watch a five-year-old. Really look at him while he plays and works. He is a symphony of movement and of sound—unless he has heard too many stern warnings to be quiet, to behave, to "act his age" and not be a "baby." This is his age.

What happens to him in kindergarten? Kindergarten is a great adventure for the child. It is usually his first experience away from home. It is his first experience with a large group of children for a whole day or half-day on a regular basis. It is his first experience, on a large scale, in becoming accepted by others because of who he is and what he does, not because he is part of a fond family. It is his first experience in learning away from home.

The baby is growing up visibly now.

What about this place in which he spends so many of his waking hours?

WHAT IS A KINDERGARTEN?

Let's consider that question carefully. A kindergarten is a strategic portion of the elementary school years devoted to the five-year old youngster. In the kindergarten he is guided by a professionally trained teacher. He is surrounded by the equipment and materials, indoor and outdoor space geared to his needs at this fifth year of life. The program encompasses all of the traditional subject-matter such as reading, writing, arithmetic, science. It does this in its own unique way based upon what we know of the child at this stage of life. The program also encompasses areas which we know to be equally as important for his further growth and development, such as social studies, the language arts, recreation, health, physical education, the humanities.

Doesn't he just play all day? That may seem to be the case, for he certainly is not rooted to a chair and desk for any length of time. He sits sometimes, as in the work period when he is busy with a project, or in story time when he is enthralled with a book that has colorful pictures and a fascinating plot. He sits when he listens to music, especially music with words that tell a story. He draws and works with clay, puzzles, scissors and paste, and construction paper. However, even when he sits, he sits actively. Everything seems to move, even though he stays in one spot—or approximately in one spot. This is a characteristic of the five-year-old. But he has lots of company. Other fives are wrigglers, too, who find it difficult to stay in one spot for long.

That is one reason a lot of activity goes on in the good kindergarten. At certain times during the kindergarten day the youngster will circulate freely and be able to join in block building activities, painting at the easel, dramatic play in the housekeeping corner, and in the sandbox, construction with wood and tools, experimenting with science equipment and materials. Outdoors in a special area he will vigorously join in the game activities with the teacher and the group. He will join other kindergarten youngsters at the much favored Jungle Jim, sandbox, and swings. He also enjoys using boxes, boards, wagons, tricycles, kegs, wheelbarrows, the seesaw, and the sliding board.

Another reason lots of activity goes on in the good kindergarten is that learning itself is not a passive process. It is an active process. The good kindergarten program recognizes this by allowing for creative activity, play, dramatization, firsthand observation, experimentation, and utilization of the child's five senses. The universal interest of children in doing, in exploring, is an ally of education. The good kindergarten program recognizes this and incorporates it.

Just what else does the good kindergarten program do? What is its role? Let's take a look at this "good" kindergarten program.

Role of the Kindergarten

The kindergarten program helps to promote and maintain the child's health and physical development.

The youngster will be able to use his large muscles in active play outdoors in the fresh air, as well as indoors with special equipment and materials. He will rest when he is tired on mats or cots. Activity alternates with quiet work and play. The danger of his becoming overtired is lessened because of this rhythm of rest, work, and play. It is also lessened because the periods are kept relatively short, with reduced stress upon small muscle activity and close work. Good nutrition and good eating habits are practiced in snack time or mid-morning lunch, as well as discussed.

The kindergarten program gives a child the opportunity to further his contact with other children and adults.

His circle of acquaintances has widened now from a few playmates living nearby to a school room filled with youngsters of similar age, his teacher or teachers, other teachers in the building, school nurse, the principal, the custodian, the bus driver. He is one among many. He must learn to share, to cooperate, to wait his turn. These are important learnings. He is more ready now at five to undertake these learnings in a small group, in larger groups, and activities which the day holds. Teacher guidance and supervision help him.

The kindergarten program provides a rich environment for living, thinking and learning.

The richer and more stimulating a child's school environment, the more certain it will be that he will learn the three R's better when the right time comes.

This rich environment will include an abundance of firsthand experiences, and a wide variety of equipment and materials suited to the child's needs in this period of his life. This environment, in order to be rich and stimulating, also will include the necessary space, freedom and time in which to explore, test, experiment, see, hear, feel, taste, and smell. However, the raw materials, important as they are, cannot come to life without an atmosphere in the school room which not only allows questions and wonderings, but welcomes them. A friendly, relaxed, accepting environment is inviting to growth. But a child who is upset and unhappy because of demands that are too big for him, is not free to wonder. He is too full of worry to follow his curiosity in search of answers.

The foundation for the three R's or reading, writing, and arithmetic, is cultivated in the kindergarten.

This foundation is cultivated by means of the readiness program. Readiness is another way of saying that the stage is set, the curtain raised and the show ready to begin. Before this grand opening, or "teachable moment," much behind-the-scenes effort has been going on. The kindergarten readiness program may be compared to the behind-the-scenes effort to prepare the youngster for the "teachable

Building the foundation for the three R's.

moment," or the grand opening of the show. This grand opening may take place some time during the kindergarten year, but the results may not be evident until the following grades in the school. However, this should not imply that the readiness program in the three R's is merely a preparation for the development of future skills. It is preparation, but the kind that needs full living right now, in accordance with what a child is able to do right now, at this particular point in his development. It includes firsthand experiences to form a background for the symbols he will bump into throughout his life. Words are actually symbols. Numbers are symbols, too. A symbol is a nothing until it means something to somebody. A symbol is dead and lifeless until somebody recognizes it. Experiences are the keys which help unlock the meanings behind symbols. The youngster is learning about symbols in the kindergarten in the way which has most meaning for him—by living the symbols. He lives the words *zoo, train, circus, pet, friend, play, happy, trip, store, farm, animals, bus, picnic, ride* when he experiences them firsthand. Words come alive because he and the other children have had an exciting trip to the nearby train station, and they are all anxious to tell what they have seen and heard. They make up a story about their trip, while teacher writes it on chart paper. The words come alive because this really happened. It happened to them. They "read" it together again, and maybe afterward one or two, or more, will ask to have individual words repeated, or will even recognize a word or words by themselves.

Words also come alive when he hears a favorite story read about children just like himself, or about animals, or pets, or trains, or fire engines. Words come alive when he sees them under a colorful big picture, or an illustration of a beloved story. Words also come alive when his drawing or painting is labeled with a sentence of his own choosing. He may recognize the words *paint, crayons, scissors, table, chair, book, paste, window, door* because these are objects which he uses and sees and the teacher has put little signs on them. He may recognize his name because his teacher pasted it above his cubby, or his locker, or his shelf where he keeps his things. He may learn to print his name because he can hold a pencil quite well for a short while and he is anxious to label his own work.

He lives the number symbols one, two, three, four, five, six, seven, eight, nine, ten when he counts straws, when he counts napkins, when he counts noses, when he counts crackers, when he counts out needed construction paper and discovers he needs another for Jane and more for Billy and John. He lives the number symbols when he compares size, when he shares equally what he has, when he matches one to one, when he measures the milk for the cookie recipes, when he solves the problem of how many children can paint at the available easels, and how many brushes they will need so that each color has its own brush. He understands the word and the number symbols because he uses them in concrete ways and because he lives them.

The kindergarten program provides opportunities for the child to expand language as a means of communication and expression.

Originality in the expression of a child's own thought is the goal in language, whether this expression is by means of words, pictures, or dramatization. He has many opportunities to express himself to other children, to small groups, to teachers, to the whole group. He expresses himself in conversation time when he shares his experiences and sometimes a favorite toy from home. He expresses himself in dramatic play in the housekeeping corner, and in play with puppets. He likes to repeat rhymes and jingles and poetry introduced by the teacher. He communicates when he exchanges ideas, when he plans with teacher and the group, when he solves problems, when he discusses, comments, questions, remarks, chants. He not only has opportunities to communicate and express himself, but listens to others in audience situations, listens to the teacher when it is her turn, and waits his turn to speak. He listens during story time, and tells stories himself about the pictures in books. All of these experiences and opportunities help him to gain the ability to collect his thoughts and express what he is thinking. They help to develop his vocabulary, his sentence structure, and his poise.

These experiences and opportunities improve his ability to listen, to hear, and to follow simple directions.

The child's understanding of the social world is broadened.

A child is interested in his world. He asks questions—endlessly, it seems. But there is a difference now. Earlier he asked questions, too. He hardly waited for the answer, though, and lost interest when the explanation was too long, or too complicated, or too dull. Now he really wants to know, and "pesters" until he has an answer satisfying to him. Or he rummages about in his world until he finds an answer which is satisfying for the time being.

The good kindergarten program recognizes a child's urge to find out. It also recognizes that he most wants to find out about his immediate environment, or living space. He brings impressions with him from his four or five years of living. These previous impressions as well as new impressions, both simple and complex, need sorting out and interpretation. The good kindergarten program realizes that a child's world is broadened by this sorting-out, finding-out, and putting-together process. It takes time, needs help, and requires opportunities for many real experiences. It also calls for understanding and skilled guidance.

The child's social world is broadened by direct contact with the school personnel and the school plant itself. It is widened by opportunities for many real experiences outside the school, such as trips to points of interest in the community. It is strengthened by hearing stories about other children of other lands and how they live, by discussing their own homes and families, and how we help one another. To foster further understanding of the world around him a youngster has the opportunity to live, play, and work with children who have a different skin color as well as different capacities, different backgrounds, and diverse experiences. All of this is part of his learning. It takes time, it needs help, it requires skilled guidance. It takes plenty of the right kind of opportunities to investigate and to grow in his five-year-old way.

The child's understanding of the scientific world is broadened.

He brings with him the most important ally of further understanding and further growth: curiosity. This curiosity, or want-to-know, is very real. It causes a child to want-to-do. This curiosity is the trigger which starts the finding-out, sorting-out, and putting-together process. This curiosity, then, is the biggest ally of education. The process of finding-out, or discovery, sorting-out or analysis, and putting-together or synthesis, is not completed in the kindergarten year, of course. It can continue all through life. The word "can" is used advisedly, for it can continue if curiosity remains alive, and is not smothered by too much pressure, or too much tension.

The kindergarten program gives a child the time and opportunity to express his curiosity in questioning, in exploration, in experimentation. Many of the answers about the scientific world necessarily will be partial ones. But even partial answers can ultimately lead to the whole. And a child's appreciation is heightened with exposure to a variety of topics.

In his study of nature, the youngster's powers of observation are being cultivated during his important early years when he is highly curious. He is being taught to consider that plants and animals are friends and helpers whose ways can be learned by observation. He is being helped to see domestic animals as helpers that deserve both care and consideration. It is not likely that a cow may be found in the child's kindergarten room, but a wide variety of other animals will. Domestic animals, pets, fish, frogs and insects are as much a part of the kindergarten as the light fixtures and the window shades. The plant world has its representatives in the kindergarten room also, in the form of the outdoor garden or window box, potted plants, and a terrarium. The representatives of both the plant and animal kingdom are as varied as the fertile brains of the children and the teacher, and as numerous as the size of the room will allow. The emphasis is where it rightfully belongs: On care and observation, and on function rather than structure.

The kindergarten program makes provision for satisfying aesthetic experiences for the child.

It recognizes that expressions of movement and of sound need both outlets and further rich experiences. Music and rhythmic and art experiences in the kindergarten program are designed to help a youngster express his own creativity. He sings and chants songs of his own making. He draws, models, paints, constructs, and weaves products which are satisfying to his child standards. He dances and uses rhythmic instruments in ways that mean something to him.

These aesthetic experiences in music and art are also designed to introduce the rich cultural heritage from our land and from other lands. He listens to and learns to sing songs which he can enjoy. He listens to music which he can learn to love. He learns new ways of using rhythmic instruments to make new sounds, to increase his enjoyment, to find new outlets for his expressions. He learns the feel of new media in art and experiments with familiar media.

Even though he is not yet concerned with the artistic standards which the adult world has, nor should he be, he is helped and encouraged to express his ideas artistically. He is helped and encouraged by having a wealth of stimulating experiences, time enough for creation, varied and suitable equipment and materials. He is also helped with technique. The emphasis here is not on how the child could or should do something a certain way in order to produce an acceptable product in adult eyes. The emphasis is on how he can achieve a certain end which he has in mind, with the help of simple techniques. The emphasis is on his impressions of his world rather than on the adult impressions of what he should see.

The kindergarten provides for further satisfying aesthetic experiences by having a cheerful, bright, eye-appealing room which is scaled to child's size. He sees and enjoys the carefully selected framed pictures on the walls. He enjoys and also contributes to the collection of colorful cards, photographs, pictures on the bulletin board. He enjoys the objects tastefully arranged in the room. These may be vases, dolls, puppets in costumes, figures of animals, and other artifacts brought from the teacher's own home or borrowed from the collection of a children's museum. He enjoys the picture books with their illustrations drawn from imaginary and real experiences in his world.

The kindergarten program provides opportunities for the child to develop his sense of responsibility.

The five-year old loves to be helper. If he is given tasks which are not too big or too demanding for him, he can complete them. He can experience the glow that comes from a finished job. Perhaps not well done by adult standards, but simply great by child standards. The kindergarten program recognizes this. There are jobs which need to be done daily as a part of the routine of the room. There are the coat closet and separate cubby which have to be kept neat. The coat or jacket or sweater is hung up, as are gloves, cap and scarf—not tossed in the corner. Boots and rubbers are placed neatly so that they can dry and be ready for wear. The resting mat or blanket is folded before it is put away in the cubby. There are plants to be watered, pets to be fed. There are materials and equipment to be put away when it is clean-up time. In work time, materials are used economically, and the job is done. If it is not completed in one session,—and there is usually enough time allotted—it can be carefully put away and completed the next time. There are utensils and refreshments to be distributed and then cleared away in mid-morning lunch time. There are visitors to be greeted and made comfortable.

The child gets home in the afternoon, preferably by himself, and gets his completed products home by himself. He gets to school on time in the morning. But preferably, he walks to school by himself, or rides on the school bus with the other children.

Is This Enough?

Small accomplishments, these, by adult standards. But giant steps in the direction of growth by kindergarten-child standards.

This is the crux. The good kindergarten program is an open invitation to the fives.

An invitation to growth.

NOTES

[1]Reprinted from *The Elementary School Journal* by E. L. Widmer by permission of The University of Chicago Press. Copyright 1967 by The University of Chicago Press.

Chapter 8

An Environment for Living and Learning

What is likely to happen during a good day, a good week in the early childhood setting? There will be variations, of course, dependent on the developmental levels of the children involved. But generally, these can be considered variations on a theme. A good day, a good week, whether designed for threes, fours or fives, for the disdavantaged or advantaged child, has many characteristics in common. The differences derive from the developmental levels of a particular group and their special needs, not from chronological age per se. Frank commented on the kindergarten as a source of help in overcoming poor beginnings, especially by imparting renewed self confidence and courage to the child. "It can help in replacing those early patterns that may become increasingly handicaps if not revised while the child is still capable of unlearning."[1]

There are basic ingredients which should be part of the sound beginnings for all children. They comprise the base or foundation upon which to build and extend. The ingredients for these sound beginnings are contained in the following list:

1. The early childhood program should consider the readiness of the child in determining the educational experiences to which he is exposed.
2. The environment provided for the child should consider his past experiences, as well as his present development, since children grow, build their concepts, skills, and attitudes through interaction with their environment.
3. Learning in the early childhood school should be facilitated by providing opportunities for: firsthand experiencing, activity, discovery, exploration, experimentation, and multisensory approaches.

A rich environment for living, thinking, and learning.

4. There should be a broad-base program of experiences and activities with exposure to a variety of areas in order to build a foundation for later skills, attitudes, knowledges, appreciations, and understandings. This type of program is considered more meaningful for the early childhood youngster than one concerned with verbalizations and abstractions.

5. Concept formation should be encouraged by providing a variety of firsthand and vicarious experiences, time, opportunity and materials with which to explore, play, investigate, test, and question.

6. The program should encompass opportunities for growth in many areas: language arts, numbers, aesthetic appreciations, social studies and science, as well as growth in physical, social, and emotional development.

7. Play activities should be included, since they are important for the growth and development of the young child.

8. Formalized, highly structured activities in content should not be provided, unless the child clearly demonstrates readiness for these activities, and these activities are provided on an individualized basis with instruction geared to the child.

9. Since the young child's primary frame of reference is still self, home-and-family, here-and-now, the activities in the early childhood setting should stress these areas of interest.

10. The early childhood school should provide and guide experiences in group living.

11. The early childhood school should provide opportunities for experiences in science through observation, experimentation and testing, as well as through firsthand experiences and exploration.

Let us translate these recommended ingredients into a dramatization of an actual good day for the fours and fives.

The first hasty impression of this early childhood setting to the unknowing eye may be one of noise and confusion with bodies milling about.

GREETINGS

Where is the teacher? Oh yes, over there by the door, smiling and greeting each child. "Good morning, how are you today? My what a pretty red dress. And just look, Mario brought his kitten to visit us.

Isn't he cute? And you remembered to bring a box to keep him in.
Good for you!"

The replies vary from broad smiles to, "I'm fine, and say, you
asked me that same question yesterday," and "Look, my tooth is
gone!" A sudden flurry, and an appeal from the teacher, "Does anyone here know whom this dog belongs to?"

"I know his name, but I don't know his address," confesses
Donna.

A little boy was holding his throat one morning. "Is anything
wrong?"

"Yep, it's sore. I think I must have bad breath."

Centers of Interest

The children enter this large, bright, spotless room with a sense
of anticipation. It has obviously been planned with them in mind
every step of the way. There is aesthetic appeal in the framed pictures, prints, and artifacts as well as the children's own art products
and lively bulletin board displays. All are at child's-eye-level. This
early childhood setting is, perhaps, the only child-centered oasis
remaining in a bustling, adult world.

There are friends to greet and outer layers of clothing to take off
and hang up in lockers. They look around to see what has been added
to the centers of interest.

Equipment and materials are ready for them at these various
centers of interest, or activity centers, contained in the room. They
are attractively and sturdily arranged and make important contributions to the young learner's growing understandings about his physical and social environment.

One center which is certain to be in evidence is the library-and-
language arts center. A table with attractive centerpiece and comfortable chairs, scatter rugs, shelves with class booklets and scrap-
books, record player and records, tape recorders and earphones, books
and magazines, puzzles and games, flannelboard with storybook cut-
outs, teacher-and-children-made puppets of all kinds are easily ac-
cessible. There are action shots of the children on the bulletin board
with captions underneath and also little stories obviously dictated
by the youngsters. These language arts resources exist for the express
purpose of providing an environment in which language is likely to
occur. The children will be guided in the development of both receptive and expressive language. Listening and speaking in a variety of
situations is encouraged.

The creative arts area is nearby, with its easels, large sheets of paper and water-base paints. Shelved supplies of paste, scissors, crayons, blank newsprint and construction paper, scrap and fabric boxes, clay, and cookie forms as well as a variety of other art media are found here, along with low tables which serve as work surfaces. Too, there is a special spirit. All who enter here may express themselves in their own unique way. A very personal self-expression is at the heart of these individual creations. The adult who observes must have understanding and respect for the child's product, or at least enough sensitivity not to demand, "What is it?." Teachers who respect children's feelings will phrase their questions carefully. The replies are usually fascinating and always interesting.

A group of kindergarten youngsters were creating on paper one day in response to the teacher's suggestion to, "Draw or paint a picture of something that makes you happy." They gathered together afterward to talk about their creations. There were pictures of families, toys, favorite foods, friends. One little fellow had drawn something quite different. It was a black rectangle and what appeared to be black grass inside it. He held it up for the teacher to see. She responded wisely with this open-ended question: "Tell me about it, Kenny."

He looked at it very seriously and replied, "I really don't know what it is. I never saw it before in my life."

The rules in operation at this center are few and clearly understood. They center around respect for the materials as well as a good neighbor policy among the creators.

The building area is strategically located away from the quieter atmosphere generally pervading the library and creative arts centers. Building and constructing is another form of expression with creatively challenging materials. Clarification of concepts and extension of understandings are encouraged here, as in all the centers of interest. There is space for vigorous building and constructing. Low shelves with a profusion of blocks of different size and shape, animal and people toys, wheel and machinery toys, small wooden carpenter's horse and in a separate corner, a wooden workbench with tools for carpentry can be seen.

Children's consuming interest in the physical world is much in evidence in the science corner where the articles on tables, shelves, and floor range from bird nests, shell and rock collections, plants, live amphibious and land creatures, levers, pulleys and ramps to sound gadget boxes, feeling books, magnets, magnifying glasses, old clocks, microscope, thermometer, wheels. The collection is as wide as the children's broad interests and the teacher's ingenuity can furnish plus gleanings from various secondhand shops, junk shops, and parental and community offerings. The children are free to make firsthand discoveries here at the science center with the materials and specimens for observation, manipulation, and experimentation. A teacher described the valuable learnings this area offered her group:

> If visitors find our science table a bit disorderly by adult standards, it is because it is not merely a place to exhibit collections but also a place to work, to play and to experiment with materials continually accessible to the children. If visitors find our interests bewilderingly scattered by adult standards, it is because the method we find most comfortable is not one of exhaustive research in any one area. We take ideas as far as we can without belaboring them and are continually returning when we discover new materials or new questions to fit in or to reject.
>
> The science work area evolved from the interests of the children with the teacher throwing in supplementary materials. Like some mythical or science fiction organism it grew, spreading its tentacles along the window sill. . . . It reached out across the wall. . . . It reached under the table. It even spilled over onto the floor. Every time we cut off a limb of exploration, it seemed to grow in another direction. Clearly, some compromise was called for if things were to be kept within bounds. The children were discovering that chaos is not useful, that too much is not even fun, that it could be a burden in cleaning up even with our minimum standards that after use things be left readily available to the next person. If there is to be order then there must be some limit, even though it is difficult to order the infinite. The teacher suggested that it seemed reasonable that they should have what they could manage. How about discarding the things they used or enjoyed least? And so it came about that there was a continual sluffing off of the unused part in order to make room for the new, thus keeping the whole a growing, living thing rather than having it become the victim of its own vitality.

A number activity center is available where the children can manipulate a variety of concrete objects ranging from nuts, toothpicks, clothespins and empty spools to small blocks, counting sticks, Cuisenaire rods, abacuses, wooden geometric shapes, designs and insets, fraction disks, balances, and weights. Experience in manipulating objects in a variety of ways is important for young children's developing mathematical concepts.

The early childhood youngster enjoys fantasy play in which he pretends to be someone or something else, perhaps an adult, or an animal, or another child. The housekeeping center of interest is literally a child-scaled miniature world in which these children can play out real-life and fantasy roles, and in the process discover themselves. It contains child-size kitchen, bedroom and living room articles of furniture and accessories as well as dress-up clothes, costumes, and community-helper uniforms which can all be used as props for the child's dramatic play episodes. The listening, watchful adult can learn to understand children better and find more ways of helping them through observation of their activities and use of the props for play found here.

A sand table, an area for water play, cooking facilities, sink and storage area for mats or cots complete the activity centers in this room. A veritable smorgasbord of children's delight, indeed! A word of caution is in order here. The wise teacher does not expose or display all the wares continuously. Careful choice plus substitution, rotation and replenishment of materials and equipment are indispensable to any purposeful, ongoing program.

Opening Exercises

When all the children have arrived, and are ready to begin their day, teacher gives a signal and they gather together for the opening exercises. These activities vary, but generally include flag salute, a song, discussion of the weather, the day of the week and the month. Possible implications arising from this may involve suitable clothing to wear, seasonable activities in which families engage, the different foods now available.

Children share experiences together in the sharing-time, or conversation-time segment of this opening period. They learn to listen when it is someone else's turn to speak, to express their ideas so that others can understand them. Indeed, these are the first beginnings of language development and public-speaking skills. It is also a prime opportunity for the adult to tune in on the child's-eye-view of the world, the budding concepts, the misconceptions, and possible areas of concern.

A wise and wonderful teacher of fours and fives announced, after a particularly lively discussion over some seeds and a balloon early in September, "Let's meet everyday like this, and then if anyone has found out anything he thinks especially interesting about the world, he can tell it or show it at this time. You know, if you find a peculiar kind of bug or something, or maybe an especially good way to settle an argument." Since one of the children looked puzzled she added, "That's finding out about the world, isn't it? Anything you see or hear or notice or find out that you think is interesting or important, come tell us. You see, there's so much to find out about, one person couldn't know it all. But if we tell each other what each discovers, well then, we could really know a lot. Right?" Children nod.

"I had a boat ride yesterday," announced loquacious, five-year-old Karen one Monday morning. "It was lots of fun."

"Did the water have wrinkles on it?" demanded Billy.

"What kind of boat was it?" asked another boy.

She thought about it.

"A row boat?" prompted Billy.

A shake of the head.

"One with a sail on it like in our story?" checked John.

Still not the right answer. Finally, a spark of illumination. "I know now," she said. "It was a secondhand boat!"

Not all children are as articulate as Karen. Some speak in incomplete sentences, in phrases, a word or two. A few do not say even a word at first. And then there are those who simply hold up an object brought from home as one little boy did, using a clean handkerchief as his contribution. The teacher does not force them to conform to any special formulas such as, "Finish the sentence," or, "That's not a story." She realizes these are beginnings, and on them hinge children's future language development. She knows they will learn to communicate in an environment rich in opportunities for all kinds of self expression, and with encouragement and understanding from her.

Hartley, Frank and Goldenson expressed it succinctly as follows:

> Even when a child does resort to speech, the adult can understand him fully only if he understands also the desires and needs from which the thought springs. Vygotsky has demonstrated that the speech of early childhood, which is egocentric speech, depends on a grammer of thought and a syntax of word meaning that are not identical with the conventional socialized speech of adults. The meaning of the child's words is derived from the whole complex of subjective experience which it arouses in him, and one word in his egocentric speech may be saturated with sense to such an extent that it would require many words in socialized speech to explain it. It follows inescapably that any teacher who would comprehend his speech and foster his growth in the social world must be continually aware of his basic affective and sensory experiences as well as his attempts at nonverbal communication.[2]

Work-Play Period

The work-play period is usually next on the schedule. There is actually no dividing line between work and play, no clear point of demarcation between the two. This is as it should be, since what appears to be play to the adult may be work in its fullest sense to the child. The absence of adult-level standards, and the constant awareness of children's own diverse learning styles and developmental levels help to give this portion of the program its meaning. Perhaps it ought to be labeled stimulation-learning period. The fact that learning proceeds throughout the whole program would make this a misnomer, however.

There is a brief discussion of any special plans and projects starting or already underway, and the choices available to the children. Teacher-group planning and individual selection are integral parts of the preparation for this portion of the program. The children may work individually and/or in small groups, or perhaps in a total group project. They may work at a special activity connected with a social studies or science unit, a planned project activity of their own, or move to a center of interest. They create artistically, build, construct, play, experiment, investigate, think, learn, and feel. There is enough flexibility and time for a child to move about, to engage in a variety of activities. There is opportunity for him to make choices as well as to join in guided activities and projects. An amusing, teacher-reported conversation relating to this work-play period is in order here.

Child: "Teacher, are we going to do work today?"

Teacher: "Why did you come to school?"

Child: "To learn how to work."

Teacher: "That's what I thought. Why did you ask?"

Child: "I'm a nut!"

At one of the low tables, Mary was cutting and pasting her project diligently. "Do you like school, Mary?" asked her teacher.

"Of course. *You're* here, aren't you?" was her reply. One of the priceless, intangible rewards of teaching, which, many teachers report, give one the will to go on.

The hum of voices heard is an encouraging sign. It indicates that these youngsters are learning to interact with one another in a meaningful work-play association. It indicates, too, that language is proceeding in the best kind of relationship for its further optimal development. Language and activity must be closely connected. There is less danger of empty verbalization, of mere parroting back what has been said without any real understanding, in an environment which capitalizes upon social interaction and activity in an experience-centered curriculum. That buzz of conversation, therefore, is a healthy sign. Real learnings are proceeding in this early childhood setting.

The work-play period is necessarily the largest block of time in the early childhood program. In order for these fours and fives to become adept at planning with teacher what they are going to do, take the necessary time to do it, evaluate afterward what they have accomplished, and clean up and clear away the materials and equipment that were in use, they need time. If this period is cut short, or if there is not enough time allotted to it, fine living-learning experiences will be wasted. It is frustrating for youngsters to become engrossed in something, and then be hurried through it or have to stop abruptly. The teacher, too, will be a loser. Opportunities to observe individual children and to give aid, encouragement, and direction will be lost in a general hurry-up and move-on atmosphere.

Outdoors

Weather permitting, outdoor play is next on the program. This is a particularly vigorous period with lots of space available for the large muscle activities of jumping, running, climbing, rolling, and swinging so enjoyed by and beneficial for fast-growing youngsters. Outdoor apparatus, large wheel and wagon toys, swings, boards and carpenter horses, packing crates, kegs and barrels, large hollow climb-through pipes, and sand box are some of the raw materials as well as structured objects in evidence at this child-centered outdoor play area. Well-spaced discussions about the few simple safety rules necessary, sufficient equipment and facilities, plus alert adult supervision will take care of any special guidance these age groups require. They are well able to teach and help one another when the occasion arises. This is well to remember in our overly safety-conscious, insurance-ridden era. A grassy, hilly playground area was being enjoyed by a group of threes, fours, and fives one windy spring afternoon. Suddenly, the writer heard a forceful, determined voice say, "No! You can't go up there." A young three had managed to slant a sturdy board against the small outdoor playhouse, and was intent on clambering up to its straight roof. This was an activity much enjoyed by the children. They were king of all they surveyed on that firm, well built roof. Wondering why this climbing foray seemed to be different, the writer watched and listened. It soon became clear. Bending down, the four-year-old explained to this recent newcomer to the group,

"First you gotta test it!" He proceeded to wiggle the base of the board back and forth on the ground until he satisfied himself that it was firmly anchored. "See? Now it's O.K."

Children can help one another very effectively. They find it easier at times to learn from one another than from an adult who cannot translate learnings into their levels of understanding.

Physical Needs

Opportunities for toileting must be as frequent as the needs of the group dictate. If the early childhood room has its own facilities, there may be no regular periods provided, instead a freedom to go and come back as necessary. If the youngsters must share the school's general facilities, then a judiciously placed, regular toileting period is in order. It is well to remember that, even though this activity may be at the bottom of a child's list of priorities in an interesting day, teacher will save all concerned trouble and embarrassment if the period is sensitively inserted with leeway allowed for individual trips.

Snack time proceeds after the outdoor activity period. The youngsters take pride in helping to serve the liquid and cookie refreshments, napkins, and straws. They take turns with the responsibilities of serving and cleaning up afterward. These are the early beginnings of a development of a sense of responsibility. Hopefully, they will have chores to do at home, too, that are within their growing abilities. This is a social time, with much small group conversation at the tables. Language development is encouraged in these natural settings, as well as incidental and planned learning experiences for the children. The teacher with listening ears can learn more about these youngsters, their interests, and developmental levels.

"That's my new boyfriend," commented a five-year-old and pointed to a boy sitting across the table from her.

"What happened to the old one?" asked her teacher.

"Oh, he's got a new girl friend, so I'm sticking to this one. For a while anyway. I'll see how this one behaves." Then, with a worried look she continued, "He doesn't live on my street. Oh well."

Rest time on cots, mats, or blankets follows. Snack and rest time constitute the pause that refreshes, and should be integral parts of the early childhood program due to the higher metabolic rate and more vigorous activity engaged in by these young, growing bodies.

Other Planned Activities

After rest time, mats, cots, or blankets are neatly folded and put away. The total group joins in activities now, such as music, rhythms, dramatization, story time, the kindergarten newspaper, special readiness activities geared to the group and to the individuals. The variety of choices possible and the planned activities available within these blocks of time will be limited by various factors. Length of the session, and the actual number of children in the group, plus room size, available facilities, equipment, materials, and trained personnel are all considerations that may force concessions in relation to optimal programming. Hopefully, there will be no more than a ratio of fifteen to eighteen children to one professionally trained adult and one aide in any group of fours, and eighteen to twenty-five children to one professionally trained adult and one aide in any group of fives. More than this will cause a curtailment of the kinds of activities that have the most educative value for this early childhood period as well as introduce dangers of overstimulation and fatigue attendant upon too many bodies being crammed into one room. A critical requirement for younger age groups as well as those containing children with learning disabilities, social and emotional problems and/or physical handicaps is to cut down appreciably on the number of children in the group and increase the adult helpers.

Whatever its length, the program is a balanced one with periods of activity and rest, with provision for physical and social needs as well as mental pursuits. The periods are generally short. When they are longer, as in the case of the work-play period, there is a variety of materials and opportunities, and a chance to move about from one center of interest to another. A young child's attention span is relatively short. Even when he is engrossed in something, he does not have the long span which he will later develop. His periods of concentration must be shorter ones because his muscles get cramped and tired from being held in one position too long, and because his eyes are not ready for concentrated, close work.

Flexibility and Routine

The program is flexible, but within this flexibility there are established routines. Some of these routines are the general periods themselves, such as opening exercises, work-play time, outdoor play, snack and rest-time, the activity periods. These periods are pegs in the kindergarten day which help to give the youngsters a sense of security.

They like to know what comes next. The author remembers a kinder-garten youngster in a group she was observing who walked up to proudly show her that he had finished all his milk. "See? All done. Do you know what I'm going to be when I grow up? A weather-man. Say, what did she (point to his teacher) say we'd do after we rinse out our milk carton and clean up the table?"

Wrinkling his brow, he considered the problem. "Oh yeah. That's right. Go to the bathroom."

Another good reason for the established routines which are a part of every good early childhood day is the physical one. The child needs the chance for mid-morning or mid-afternoon nourishment for his active body. He needs a time when he can be physically active indoors and in the fresh air, a time in which he can use his large muscles. He needs rest to repair his body tissues and give his muscles a chance to repair the effects of activity. He needs to know when he can count on getting to the bathroom.

His attempts at socialization, while very real, and very important to him are still imperfect. He still needs time and space in which to be alone. The early childhood program recognizes this and gives him op-portunities to work and play individually, beside other children, and with groups of other children. The taking of turns, the consideration for others, the sharing are learned as he lives and works and plays with other children. His occasional lapses are understood, as are his inconsistencies. He is an early childhood youngster. He has a long time to grow. He is learning.

Discipline

Discipline is usually not a problem with a normal group of young-sters. The emphasis is *where* it should be. It is on prevention by means of an adequate, balanced program, carefully selected materials and equipment and by means of supervision and guidance. The em-phasis is also on acceptance of a child for what he is, on encourage-ment, on praise, and on group approval. The emphasis is on a warm, supportive atmosphere. Excessive demands which are beyond the abil-ities and development of children have no place in the good early childhood setting. Discipline problems are at a minimum in such a growth-inducing atmosphere and environment.

Sample Schedule

Although kindergartens may fall short of their worthwhile goals in the practices they employ, well-designed programs do attempt to utilize both a wide variety of interesting and satisfying materials and experiences appropriate for early childhood youngsters. Too, care and attention is devoted to creating an atmosphere which is inviting and conducive to interpreting and assimilating experiences which have meaning for children.

Since most kindergartens convene for no more than half a day, it is well to remember that planning is more likely to be balanced and developmental in nature if carried out on a weekly rather than daily basis. A sample schedule which provides for variety within blocks of time, flexibility, balance between active and quiet periods as well as between total, small group and individual activities follows. Morning hours are listed, with the understanding that these would correspondingly change for afternoon sessions, and with the added admonition that as the children's interest waxes or wanes, the blocks of time expand and contract accordingly.

8:30– 9:45	Children arrive: Morning greetings and helper responsibilities—e.g., watering plants, feeding pets, etc.
	Conversation-sharing time.
	Work-play period: small group and individual activities, projects, choices at centers-of-interest.
	Clean-up and informal evaluation-discussion.
9:45–10:15	Large-group activities: music and rhythms, records, filmstrips, fingerplays, auditory-visual discrimination activities, and other readiness learning experiences.
10:15–10:45	The pause that refreshes: toileting, mid-morning snack and rest.
10:45–11:15	Story time, poetry, choral speaking, science exploration and experimentation, discussion of field trips, etc.
11:15–11:45	Outdoor play period, plans for next day.
	Dismissal.

NOTES

[1]Lawrence K. Frank, "A Good Beginning Has No End," *Childhood Education*, No. 36 (September 1959), p. 3.

[2]Ruth E. Hartley, Lawrence K. Frank, and Robert M. Goldenson, *Understanding Children's Play* (New York: Columbia University Press, 1952), p. 7.

Chapter 9

The Three R's in Perspective

Those who work with young children, who have the most direct contact with our young, have an awesome responsibility. The sharp focus on early childhood as a particularly critical period for educational as well as physical, social, emotional, and cognitive growth makes it imperative that we become more than just nominally acquainted with our young. Each child shows the perceptive adults in his life the areas and ways in which they can contribute to his development, if only these adults have the sensitivity to listen, and the sense to respond appropriately! Sensitivity and sense can be developed within the key adults in the child's life. The basic requirement is comprehensive understanding of child growth and development. The curriculum, methodology, practices, and materials of learning that we devise for children in our educational enterprises should be deeply and inextricably rooted in this knowledge and understanding of our children. Bobroff pinpointed the issue when he stated, "Only when educational objectives and methods are designed within the context of the sequence of development of the students can they be appropriate and effective."[1] Only with understanding of child growth and development at its base, can home and school hope to build an optimal environment for further growth and development.

We must learn to see children as they actually are and be concerned with what they can do that has value for them. We cannot view them with eyes that sharply appraise in terms of high levels of adult oriented expectations out of touch with the realities of growth and development. Some of what we expect from children today is in terms of demands, pressures, and expectations that are out of context, out of touch with the realities of growth. Keliher highlighted the heartbreaking toll which unrealistic demands are extracting from our children:

> In forty-one child suicides studied in New Jersey, not one of these children had a friend, adult or child. In some cases, the child had a parent who was saying, "You are doing better. But you must do a *lot* better." This kind of psychology is defeating. It should be a victory just to be doing better. Who are we to say how much better he should be doing?[2]

Caswell had serious doubts about these pressures:

> If lifetime productivity is considered, may it not be far better for children to have a more leisurely approach to learning so that they really can savor it, and have, when they are adults, a later age of retirement? Often, I feel sure, children in elementary and secondary school work the longest days and the longest weeks of anyone in their homes. In our affluent society, why not give our children and youth opportunity for broad learnings, as free of frustrating and limiting pressures as possible?[3]

Curricula, methods and materials which are planned and carried out with children in mind, children as part of an early childhood group, as well as unique individuals with special needs and interests, are always more vital and significant than those confined to adult-oriented standards.

Activities in the early childhood program include subjects considered "basic" by generations of adults from every segment of our culture, the three R's. The humanities, the arts, and the sciences are also integral parts of the program. The differences in the early-childhood approach as compared with that of the later levels of the elementary school lie not so much in *what* as in *how* they are covered. Emphasis is not upon acquisition of a set body of information, or even upon compartmentalizing into specific subject areas at all. The emphasis is where it should be: upon an experience-centered, activity-oriented, broad-base curriculum within a functional setting. Ausubel pointed out the advantages of the activity program for the elementary school as well:

> Many features of the activity program are based on the premise that the elementary school child perceives the world in relatively specific and concrete terms and requires considerable firsthand experience with diverse concrete instances of a given set of relationships before he can abstract genuinely meaningful concepts. Thus, an attempt is made to teach factual information and intellectual skills in the real-life functional context in which they are

Fostering growth in the communicating arts.

customarily encountered rather than through the medium of
verbal exposition supplemented by artificially contrived drills and
exercises. This approach has real merit.[4]

In describing a British infant school group of youngsters, ages
five through seven, Schlesinger noted:

> Above all, there was . . . a feeling of possibility, of interest-
> ing things waiting to be discovered. The children were busy, crea-
> tive, interested in what they were doing. The teachers gave help
> and support but left the children enough room to make the dis-
> coveries on their own. . . .
> One teacher stressed the importance of human dignity as the
> key to the creative classroom environment. . . . A creative learning
> situation demands respect for the child's individuality.[5]

THE TWO R's

The current furor over reading in the kindergarten has caused
many to lose their perspective. Reading of the printed page itself
is a high-level, complicated process involving many skills. To stop
with this description might simplify the task, but would not do
justice to the actual complexity involved. Seeing is not done with
the eyes alone. There must be stress on the unity of sensory input
since other sense modalities are also involved. And comprehension
must be at the base, or reading will deteriorate into mere word-calling. Too, there must be something more which draws the reader to
the printed page, helps him to benefit from the experience. That
something more is the much underrated joy of reading.

If the furor would localize to a concern over the lack of readers
who voluntarily turn to books as a source of pleasure and information, we would stand a better chance of developing a new generation
of avid readers. Unfortunately, the emphasis seems to be on early
exposure to the mechanical, skill aspects of reading and the earlier
the better. We have the cart before the horse. Immersion in the
beauty, the delight, the wonder, pathos, and sheer power of words
is the kind of early exposure children need. This is the most produc-
tive and fruitful exposure.

Holt pinpointed the issue:

> Our so-called best schools are turning out students most of
> whom, in any real and important sense, are as inarticulate as the
> most deprived children of the ghettos, as little able to speak or
> write simply and directly about things of importance to them, what

they know, want, and care about. . . .

What we have to recognize is something quite different, that it is the effort to use words well, to say what he wants to say, to people whom he trusts and wants to reach and move, that alone will teach a young person to use words better . . . we must begin from here or we will make no progress at all.[6]

Strickland emphasized that the first task of the kindergarten teacher is to encourage the children to talk by providing time and experiences. The language program can only begin with the children themselves within a stimulating environment. "Children would not learn to talk if there were not people to talk to and things and experiences to talk about. Interesting things to do, look at, handle, arrange and make motivate children to talk."[7]

To expect the early childhood youngster to achieve competence in the language arts within a definite period of time is another unrealistic demand. Language acquisition is developmental in nature. It cannot be standardized. For example, some youngsters may comfortably learn the more formal skill aspects of reading in the kindergarten, while others may not be ready for this until later. In some cases, not until much later. Danger lies in blanket rules which demand a certain level of reading or of language performance from all kindergarten youngsters. There is danger in blanket rules of any kind. They may apply to a sterile, scientific laboratory context, but not to the growing child. We can perhaps make one absolute blanket rule: individual differences will be found whenever two or more children are brought together. Ilg stated that growth is a complex of three forces: age, individuality, and environment. Each must be considered separately and also together with the other two. Only then are we in a position to help a child to grow in his own unity.[8]

We can also add that language and action must go hand in hand in any program designed to encourage language development. Language is meaningless without both adequate and suitable experience; conversely, experience takes on deeper meaning with language both as outlet and expression. In planning a stimulating environment replete with many opportunities for language development, then, consideration of the following must be ever-present: the kind of home environment a child brings with him to school, the developmental level on which he is functioning and coping, and his own special mode of learning. As Holt emphasized, the natural learning that a child does in his own way tends to serve his purposes best.[9]

Highly structured methods imposed from without are more

likely to lead to frustration and failure than to accomplishment since they are not geared to a youngster's own style of learning. It is well to remember during any period of agonizing reappraisal and upheaval in education, that there are youngsters who teach themselves to read quite successfully, and without benefit of any of our so-called indispensable methods and materials. Interestingly, and surely not coincidentally, it occurs before formal school attendance.

Almy's implications for beginning reading instruction emerged from Piaget-inspired research on concept formation. Neglect in providing many and varied concrete experiences in the period of preoperational thought, it appears, may later hinder the child's development of abstract thinking, and possibly may interfere with the development of reading comprehension itself. It becomes the adult's role to design the environment so that the child is exposed to many and varied sensory and motor experiences, people who share activities with him, and who read and talk with him.[10] According to Greenbaum, the child is beginning to read when he hears us speak and recognizes the sounds which the letters make.[11]

Lewis's primary purpose in her doctoral study was to measure the ability of beginning kindergarten children to perform auditory and visual discrimination skills. This study is particularly noteworthy, since these skills should be well established prior to systematic instruction in the area of language arts. She concluded that, although the average kindergarten children were able to hear the rhyming element in words, the majority of them experienced considerable difficulty in hearing the beginning sounds in words. The children also experienced more difficulty in making letter and word discriminations than in making geometric designs and pictures.[12]

Based upon her observations in other countries as well as experience in the United States, Strickland remarked that far more evidence is needed that we now have to justify universal teaching of reading to five-year-old youngsters.[13] Indeed, our hastening youngsters through their developmental stages in order to force the maturational and developmental process has no basis in fact. Instead, there is considerable evidence which suggests that any momentary gains resulting from artificial hothouse, pressure-cooker environments are not permanent. Mental hygienists reiterate the theme that "the best guarantee of a normal maturity is a normal immaturity."[14]

There is a positive relationship between length of kindergarten

and high academic achievement in elementary school, declared Brubaker, The schools she studied stressed experience, readiness, and
social adjustment in their kindergarten program. It is interesting to
note that no attempt was made to teach the subjects which are
measured by achievement tests. [15]

There is additional research which supports the view that a sound
experience-centered program in kindergarten has long-range benefits
for the development of reading and for language development as well
as other subject areas. In addition, Fuller summarized that careful,
scientifically controlled research does not support the use of formalized
reading exercises in kindergarten. Nor is there any definitive proof
that early forced feeding of the more formal aspects of reading involving heavy use of symbols, drill, and workbook-type activities results
in long-lasting aims. It can and has resulted in children who avoid
reading like the plague if given a choice in the matter. This does
not, however, condone omission of reading experiences: "Such evidence and experiences as we have points to individualizing reading
with instruction adjusted to the child's general maturation level and
attitude toward reading."[16] Smith concluded that the kindergarten
teacher has a responsibility to give meaning to reading symbols—not
through the use of basal reader materials, but through abundant contacts with these symbols in meaningful situations.[17] And herein lies a
tale. Capable, conscientious kindergarten teachers have provided
these kinds of experiences for their children for many years as part of
a carefully planned development-oriented, child-centered program.
They have been remiss, however, in adequately explaining and "selling" their important goals and practices to the community and to
their frequently uninformed local boards of public instruction. Public relations is an integral aspect of any alert, concerned early childhood teacher's role, and contributes to the success of a well-designed
language-arts program, or any program, for that matter.

Written language is the natural outgrowth of an environment
in which exciting happenings are the order of the day. What more
logical progression than to "write down" emotion-arousing occur-
rences as another form of sharing and as a way of preserving experience for all to savor again and again. Teacher is ever ready to assume
the role of secretary for individual children and the total group. Too,
active living requires lists, charts, and labels for remembrance, for
guideposts, and for fun. Printing one's own name after seeing it

on dozens of occasions, and after becoming more adept at controlling the small muscles in the hand is another natural progression which needs no special emphasis or forced feeding.

THE LAST R

Piaget's and Inhelder's research has shown that young children do not understand cardinal number values, nor the ordinal position of a number in a series. Until these concepts are understood, then, the process of adding and subtracting cannot be clear. This understanding seems to develop at about seven and a half years.[18]

Inhelder's experiments demonstrated that children more easily form basic arithmetical-geometrical ideas when introduced to manipulation at an early age, and continue to have manipulative experiences.

> If, however, experimentation is introduced before the child can generalize, he will not gain insight. Given an appropriate experiment at the suitable age and not earlier, children can come to understand the concepts of invariability more easily, move through the stages of mathematical development faster, and deduce general principles more readily. In a study of the mathematical development of children from nine to eleven years of age, Inhelder discovered how much learning occurred while her subjects experimented with the materials presented to them. Manipulations greatly aided their insights at that age.[19]

It seems that manipulation aids the learning process during the middle years of childhood as well. Wohlwill demonstrated qualitative and quantitative aspects of concept formation in his report.

> In the period age 4 to 7 Wohlwill discerned three stages in the conceptualization of number: perceptual, symbolic, and superordinate comprehension of relationship. These were seen as a continuum along a cumulative scale.[20]

From the many experiments which Piaget, Inhelder, and others have performed, it is evident that young children do not, and indeed cannot, evolve mathematical concepts, nor can they derive concepts in the language arts or in any other subject area, by manipulation of symbols, by verbalizations, or by mechanical processes.

Children gain concepts through manipulation of actual concrete objects, and through opportunities for classification of objects, arranging them in different patterns, putting them in a series and in one-to-one correspondence. These, then, are the developmental kinds of learnings which build a base of understanding for children's later dealings with mathematical symbols.

Fuller brought perspective to bear on the whole exposure-mastery controversy:

> One facet of the exposure-mastery question, with regard to the kindergarten curriculum, is the necessity of exposing five-year-olds to a broad and varied sample of the content of many subject-matter fields. Since most kindergartens convene for no longer than 2 to $3\frac{1}{2}$ hours daily, devoting regular portions of the day to set and formal instruction in a single subject (such as reading or numbers) automatically deprives other subjects of their fair share of attention.[21]

SOCIAL STUDIES EXPERIENCES

A major goal in these early childhood years is to help the child to broaden his social environment through guided opportunities to live, play, and work with other children of various backgrounds and experiences. He needs to begin thinking in terms of otherness rather than just me-ness. The conflicts which naturally arise as part of these beginning social experiences are recognized as important learnings in the long process of understanding live-and-let-live considerations.

"Susie pushed you? I know you're upset, but why don't you tell her how you feel? You can use words instead of fists."

"Mike won't let you see his truck? Well, do you think you could make him feel friendly toward you? That might help. We usually like to show things to our friends."

Young children need guidance in developing understandings about how to live together with consideration for the rights of others. They also need opportunities to try to work through solutions to the inevitable conflicts which arise. The wise, watchful adult on the sidelines realizes that it is only through experience that they can learn, but must step in when temperatures are at the boiling point and the situation is clearly out of hand.

The housekeeping unit can be an important means of facilitating social development as well as providing fertile ground for spontaneous conversation and guided discussions, role playing, and dramatic play. Carefully selected, child-size equipment and toys are actually the props of a human relations laboratory. There are rich opportunities here for early childhood learnings such as sharing, taking turns, working and playing in large and small group situations, and living within some well-defined restrictions.

General themes to be explored are living in the home, at school, in the neighborhood and community, all within the framework of the interdependence of man. There are large meanings, indeed, but can be understood by the young child within the context of his dependence upon parents, siblings, classmates, teachers, other school personnel, neighborhood and community helpers. The child's home-based horizons should also be stretched to include new understandings about children of other lands; what they eat, the games they play, the stories they listen to, the songs they sing, the clothing they wear, the kind of lives they lead, and the activities they enjoy. For the young child to understand these concepts they must be presented within the framework of his style of learning, which include dependence upon a multisensory approach, direct and vicarious experiences, and active involvement in his immediate environment.

Trips are planned as part of the child's growing discoveries of a wider world outside the home and school building—the community. Powers of observation are sharpened by discussions of the anticipated excursion, as well as group evaluations of what was seen, heard, felt, and learned on the trip itself. Resources within the neighborhood and community provide firsthand learnings about the world around the child.

The aims and objectives of the social studies program, then, encompass areas critical for the young child's further growth and development. These can be stated as follows:

1. Develop understandings of cooperative group living with an awareness of and appreciation for the rights of others, personal property, honesty, courtesy, responsibility.

2. Broaden the child's social environment through guided opportunities to live, play, work, and meet with other children and adults of various backgrounds, religions, and races.

3. Explore the child's here-and-now interests in his environment, focusing on home, school and neighborhood; stress the interdependence of man in neighborhood and community.

4. Aid the child's understanding of his dependence upon parents, older siblings, teachers, school personnel, neighborhood and community helpers, and how he can help others.

5. Stretch the child's horizons to include new understandings relating to children in other countries of the world and their ways of living.

These are the important early beginnings of concept formation. Learnings become meaningful to the early childhood youngster in a stimulating school environment which provides diverse sensory-manipulative experiences and a breadth of purposeful activities. His here-and-now concerns are used as a base from which to build up to new understandings and interests in his ever-expanding social world.

SCIENCE IN AN EARLY CHILDHOOD SETTING

Young children's keen interest in their surroundings, their desire to handle things, to take them apart, their fascination with the changes observed in plant life, animals, seasons, and science phenomena in general constitute a built-in, ready-made science curriculum for the alert teacher.

The groundwork for future scientific understandings is laid in these early years through an experimental, observational approach to the child's hows, whys, and whats concerning the physical world. There will be partial answers supplied through these direct, firsthand science experiences and the opportunities to handle concrete science materials. The young child is not interested in complete, detailed, complex answers, nor is he yet ready for these kinds of understandings. With specialization comes exclusion. He is not ready for specialization. He needs to explore all kinds of experiences which do not aim to give him complete knowledge, but which do lay a foundation for the scientific approach. This early questioning and investigating is the prelude to the more selective data-collecting and sophisticated scientific inquiry which is developed during the middle years of childhood and particularly during adolescence.

During the early childhood years, realistic overall goals for the science program may be stated as follows:

1. To develop beginning concepts and sharpen the child's powers of observation.
2. To provide a broad-base approach to the science curriculum rather than specialization in any one area.
3. To use an experimental, let's-find-out, problem-solving approach to discovering meanings behind natural processes and phenomena observed in the environment.

4. To give a scientifically accurate and truthful picture within the actual areas of exploration and within the child's range of comprehension and readiness.
5. To provide answers to the child's questions that will be satisfactory to his present levels of readiness and understanding.
6. To encourage the development of appreciation and wholesome attitudes toward the wonders of the physical world around him.
7. To encourage the child's appreciation of plants and animals as friends and helpers who deserve respect and care.
8. To stimulate further curiosities and interests.

The teacher's role in developing a science program that has meaning for these children is a critical one. Too often have teachers expressed fears that they are "just not up to developing a curriculum in the science area. I'm scared to death of it." As in any area, an individual brings with him his previous experience to each new situation. We cannot be expected to know everything. But the very realistic expectation does exist that we admit our gaps in understanding and set about rectifying our shortcomings. This requires additional study, plus an ever-present let's-find-out-together, investigative zeal. He who would be a teacher must also be a learner. The two go hand in hand in any meaningful endeavor.

The teacher's responsibilities in the development of a vital science program for the fours and fives are similar to the development of any meaningful program:

1. Acquisition of sufficient background knowledge about the subject under inquiry to make it a worthwhile learning experience.
2. Development of competency in interpreting information within the early childhood levels of comprehension, and sensitivity to know how to use it to fulfill present curiosities and stimulate new interests.
3. Advanced planning, including any initial preparation and experimentation with materials, before introducing the experience to the children.
4. Awareness of the importance of children's own efforts to investigate and experiment, and provision for frequent manipulative, exploratory experiences.
5. Allowance of ample time for individual experimentation, manipulation, and exploration.

6. Selection of aids to make experiences more meaningful—equipment, illustrations, books, magazines, pictures, films, filmstrips, recordings, excursions, and other relevant activities and materials.

7. Careful evaluation of the program in terms of overall, long-range goals as well as special, short-range objectives for a present group of children.

A wise teacher of threes, fours and fives had this comment about the place science occupied in her program: "Science was a way of life with the nursery and kindergarten group, so familiar that it never occurred to us to dignify it with its formal title in order that the outside world might understand its importance. . . . We used to allude to it as 'finding out about the world.'"

What are the best means of planning for social studies and science learnings during these early years? Just as there is no one best approach, there is also no best time of day that should be reserved, with an eye on the clock. It is, rather, a natural capitalizing upon children's interests in their environments, upon opportunities arising from spontaneous incidents, on problems arising from group endeavors. Incidental as well as planned experiences are utilized. The teacher's own interests, enthusiasms, and special strengths provide another legitimate source of social studies and science experiences, as well as deliberately planned explorations centering around the children's immediate environment.

The outstanding early childhood program is concerned with growth in many areas. These concerns include reading, writing, arithmetic, language arts, aesthetic appreciations, social studies and science, as well as growth in physical, social, and emotional development. This is a broad-base curriculum with exposure to a variety of areas. It is a good foundation upon which to build later skills, attitudes, knowledges, appreciations, and understandings. Formalized activities in content as such should not be provided, unless the child clearly demonstrates readiness, and unless these activities are provided on an individualized basis with instruction geared to the child.

RECURRING THEMES

The recurring themes which ought to underscore the early education of all children include:

1. A supportive, encouraging atmosphere with development of a positive self-concept at its core.
2. An enriched environment with a range of multisensory opportunities for experiencing plus ample time within the framework of a broad-base curriculum.
3. A broadly trained teacher who understands children, readiness factors, curriculum, methodology, and materials thoroughly and always plans with a current group of children as the primary determiner of program.
4. Provisions for play activities by means of equipment, materials, time, and space.
5. The importance of the group and the group climate in the social, emotional, physical, and cognitive development of children.
6. The curiosity and interests of children as valuable resources for the educative process.
7. A balanced program with provisions for active periods alternating with quiet periods, physical needs for large-muscle activity, rest, nourishment, fresh air.

In such a setting, the court of first and last resort is the young learner himself.

Screening Is in Order

We must carefully screen the curricular materials, manuals, guides, paraphernalia, and gadgets with which we are being inundated. If these approaches rely mainly upon formal academic requirements, upon subject-matter achievement, or upon conditioned learning responses characteristic of animals in laboratory settings, then beware. Contrary to what enthusiasts claim, these are just one aspect of the broad vista of thinking, learning, and becoming.

Responses arrived at through conditioned learning are achieved with the help of various highly structured approaches. These range from the more simple workbooks, kits, packaged learning devices, to the more complex programmed and computer-based technological devices which are enjoying ascendancy in some areas able to afford them. It is no loss if these are beyond the means of a school district. School money would be better spent on salaries and incentives for outstanding teachers who have the basic understandings derived from educational background, training, and intelligence, plus the creativity to devise meaningful learning environments with a specific, current group of youngsters always in mind.

Materials have meaning for young children only if based upon their current and very real interests, needs, and concerns. It is the learning process which should be of major concern, not the product. Those who place heavy emphasis upon subject-matter achievement and the indiscriminate use of machines, gadgets, kits and workbooks are guilty of perpetrating meaningless verbal learnings, memorization and regurgitation on cue. These kinds of end products are insignificant and should not be tolerated in thoughtful educational enterprises specifically designed for early childhood youngsters.

READINESS FACTORS

The importance of readiness in the learning process of young children—in fact, all learners at any age—must not be underestimated if our curricula are to have any meaning. Learning is facilitated by a consideration of the factors of readiness. Ausubel summarized its importance well:

> There is little disagreement about the fact that readiness always crucially influences the efficiency of the learning process and often determines whether a given intellectual skill or type of school material is learnable at all at a particular stage of development. . . . Readiness—the idea that attained capacity limits and influences an individual's ability to profit from current experience or practice—is empirically demonstrable and conceptually unambiguous.[22]

There are differences of opinion concerning readiness as an active process of preparation versus readiness as a process of waiting-for-something-to-happen. A first-grade teacher who subscribed to the latter approach was found, after considerable difficulty, knitting in the only quiet corner of her classroom in late September.

"What are you doing?" inquired the perspiring supervisor who had been vainly trying to establish order in the midst of the bedlam being created by twenty-eight six-year-olds.

With a calm engendered by sincere belief, the young woman replied, "I'm waiting."

"Yes?" encouraged the supervisor. One had to admire the firm dedication which kept both her voice volume and wrath down.

"They're not ready for anything yet. So I'm just waiting."

Unfortunately, history does not record the ensuing conversation.

While maturation is certainly an integral part of readiness, so, too, is active provision for stimulating experiences and awareness of the importance of the "teachable moment."

The ever-present question of when a child should learn academic skills heavily dependent upon form and symbol recognition receives differing reactions. Some claim that the child should start young in order to be ahead of the game. They cite evidence to support their contention that it is possible to teach children of nursery school age academic skills. Others reiterate that this so-called early gain may not be a gain at all, since studies have not conclusively demonstrated lasting effects in youngsters exposed to early forced feeding. They ask if it would not, indeed, be better for this young child to be spending his childhood in ways more conducive to his optimum growth and development. Olson affirmed that, "The error that people make is in assuming that if they start teaching they will create readiness and develop skill in the child. Such instruction is met by disinterest and avoidance on the part of the child who is not ready."[23]

Fortunately, children have some built-in safeguards. They find ways to escape our excessive demands. Sometimes these may include the harmless though irritating symptoms which are contained in the label "daydreamer." The "underachiever," "dropout," or the more apt term "pushout," are other catchall phrases which actually denote the learner who has discovered a safety valve and then, a final exit out of an intolerable situation. Unfortunately, we are the losers as well as the child.

Readiness for learning activities can be determined by various means. Indicators of reading readiness were pointed out by Heffernan:

> Parents watching a child at home may observe certain behaviors which convinced them that their child is ready to learn to read. He has a wide background of experience. He enjoys having stories read or told to him. He may even be able to retell a story with a high degree of accuracy. These abilities are true indicators of reading readiness, but they are not all the indicators and they are not enough. The child must also have sufficient mental development; he must have a degree of eye coordination sufficient to focus on the printed symbol and perceive it clearly; he must have the ability to attend to symbols; he must have attained sufficient social and emotional maturation. . . .[24]

Hildreth's list of the determiners of a child's readiness is comprehensive: (1) mental maturity, (2) linguistic maturity, (3) perceptual

maturity, (4) sensory acuity, (5) social and emotional adjustment, and
(6) experience, or background.[25] Vandeburg cited goals in the area
of furthering readiness for the language arts which parallel the goals
involved in the development of readiness in general: (1) developing
favorable attitudes, (2) providing wide experiences, (3) extending concepts, (4) oral-language facility, (5) auditory discrimination, (6) visual
discrimination.[26]

Kephart provided much food for thought in this paragraph:

> It is well to stop occasionally and consider the demands which
> are made of the child for behavior adaptations. Not only is be-
> havior at a high level of achievement demanded, but such be-
> havior is demanded of an organism which has not yet completed
> the development necessary for such adaptation. Such demands are
> double-barreled: behavior is demanded on the one hand, while
> indirectly (and often knowingly) a complex learning activity is
> demanded as well. This underlying learning activity is most com-
> plex—so complex that no other species can even accomplish it, let
> alone develop efficiency.[27]

The early childhood program is the one remaining oasis in an educational desert in which the readiness-for-learning of the child is most
likely still taken into consideration in determining the program of
activities.

Perceptual Readiness

The development of perception, or the recognition of stimuli,
is at the core of our understanding of our world, and lifegiving in terms
of intellectual development. Perceptual readiness is perhaps the most
vital element in the links leading to readiness to learn anything.
There is general agreement with Getman's and Kane's statement:
"The development of the perceptual skills is related to the levels of
coordinations of the body systems; i.e., the better the coordination of
the body parts and body systems the better the prospects are for developing perception of forms and symbols."[28]

Kephart asserted that we cannot separate perceptual activities
from motor-activities and think of them as different patterns, hence
referred to these activities as perceptual-motor.[29] It is difficult, if not
impossible, for example, to discern in a tracing or copying task
what aspect is motoric and what perceptual, hence why attempt to
separate these processes at all? His theory is that the input functions,
consisting of sensory or perceptual activities, and the output functions

or motor activities of the body, move in a feedback cycle which alters and renovates responses. Thus the perceptual process itself, through this action and reaction, calls forth new cycles which contribute to further development.[30]

The young child's active exploration of his environment is familiar to those who live and work with him. What is perhaps not as well known is the fact that through this constant manipulation of objects in his environment and of his own body in relationship to these objects, this child is learning to match sensory data to motor data. Thus, he is developing flexible perceptual-motor processes, and in so doing, fitting his behavior to the demands of future situations.[31]

> Beginning very early, the child comes to perceive many aspects of the world around him. This perceptual development takes place through the sensory modalities such as vision, hearing, touch, and even taste and smell. This development continues in more and more complex ways as the child approaches the beginning of formal schooling at age six. Perceptual development is stimulated by environments which are rich in the range of experiences available; which make use of games, toys, and many objects for manipulation; and in which there is frequent interaction between the child and adults at meals, playtime, and throughout the day. . . . The typical middle-class home provides a very complex environment for the child's early perceptual development, and this gives these children some advantage in the early years of school.[32]

Each of us is a space dweller, in a sense. The development of direction, then, is important to us in our living. A child must become clearly aware of his body in relation to this space surrounding him and learn to use his body as a beginning reference point for perceptual-motor responses. It is the development of concepts of internal awareness which allows the child to then project these concepts into space as directionality.

> There are no objective directions in space. The directions which we attribute to space (right, left, up, down, before, behind, etc.) are attributed to external space on the basis of activities which take place within the organism. We do not receive from outside our organism any direct information concerning direction. When a sharp instrument is applied to the skin, there is a direct experience of pain, but there is no similar direct experience of spatial relationships and direction. Spatial clues, visual or auditory, obtain their directionality through learning and through the projection onto external stimuli or internal experiences that result from the movement of the organism.[33]

Laterality, or the internal awareness of two sides of the body and their difference within the context of surrounding space, seems to be the first direction which develops.[34] Kephart, along with other workers in this area, feels that teachers should offer the child motor activities to help him develop his awareness of his body in space and what it can do.[35] Movement and manipulation are at the basis of perceptual development and a variety of experiences help to give meaning to the child's developing perceptions.

Informed, experienced early childhood teachers have always been aware of the importance of sensorimotor activities to the child's further intellectual, social, and emotional as well as physical growth. The current research in this area merely confirms the value of these activities to the well-planned program. It appears that later achievement in formal academic skills is enhanced by this early, strong base of sensorimotor activities with emphasis properly upon the process, the doing, and not the end product. The control a child has over his body will determine the degree of his academic success.

Perceptual-motor programs list many activities that are considered helpful to the development of the child's perceptual readiness. Roach and Kephart supplied details on available materials, procedures, and evaluations.[36] Sutphin's sensorimotor approach to learning includes gross motor training, fine motor training through various manipulative activities and concept building through various experiences, including music.[37] Frostig, it seems, has not gone far enough in her program which emphasizes visual perception. She does not consider motor development as a basic foundation to perception.[38] It is well to consider these and other programs from the perspective of strengths, weaknesses and possible overemphasis upon too-structured, complicated activities. Also, there should be careful evaluation of actual results in controlled samplings as compared with groups not exposed to these special activities.

There should be concern over references to the disadvantaged child as totally lacking in any strengths useful in a middle socioeconomic school context. This is just not true. His early environment does tend to produce certain deficits in perceptual skills, according to research.[39] But these youngsters are not lacking in a very important prerequisite to readiness and learning: gross motor response. Their physical response to learning through manipulation and movement is very real and a resource to be tapped. In one recent survey, it was found that the disadvantaged children with a Head Start background did not differ significantly in perceptual-motor skill performance from a group of upper middle socioeconomic level youngsters with a kindergarten background.[40] DiMeo stressed that more investigation into the potential which perceptual-motor programs offer the young disadvantaged child is necessary.[41] Miller and Swanson concluded from studies "that if the teacher enables [children] to express themselves with the large muscles of the torso and limbs, her students may make surprising educational progress."[42]

NOTES

[1]Allen Bobroff, "The Stages of Maturation in Socialized Thinking and in the Ego Development of Two Groups of Children," *Child Development*, No. 31 (1960), p. 336.

[2]Alice V. Keliher, *What's Important in the Early Years?* Keynote Address, Florida Association on Children Under Six, Annual Conference, November 9, 1967.

[3]Hollis L. Caswell, "Difficulties in Defining the Structure of the Curriculum," *Curriculum Crossroads* (New York: Columbia University Press, 1962), p. 110.

[4]David P. Ausubel, *Human Growth and Development* (Urbana: University of Illinois, Bureau of Educational Research), pp. 9–10.

[5]Joy Schlesinger, *Leicestershire Report: The Classroom Environment.* unpublished mimeo, Fall 1966, p. 8.

[6]John Holt, "Introduction" in Herbert R. Kohl, *Teaching the "Unteachable,"* pp. 6, 7, 9. Reprinted with permission from *The New York Review of Books.* Copyright © 1967 the New York Review.

[7]Ruth G. Strickland, "The Language Arts in the Kindergarten," *Toward Better Kindergartens* (Washington, D.C.: Association for Childhood Education International, 1966), p. 56.

[8]Frances Ilg, *The Child From Three to Eight, With Implications for Reading* (Washington, D.C.: U.S. Department of Health, Education, and Welfare, Bulletin OE-30014, 1964).

[9]John Holt, *How Children Learn* (New York: Pitman Publishing Company, 1967).

[10]Milly C. Almy, *Young Children's Thinking and the Teaching of Reading* (New York: Columbia University Press, 1962).

[11]"Learning ABC's Should Come Last, Not First," *Today's Child*, Vol. 16 (February 1968), p. 1.

[12]Alice Juanita Lewis, "An Inventory of the Auditory and Visual Discrimination Abilities of Beginning Kindergarten Children" (unpublished Doctoral Dissertation, The State University of Iowa, 1959).

[13]Ruth G. Strickland, *op. cit.*

[14]Willard C. Olson, *Child Development* 2d ed. Boston: D.C. Heath and Company, 1959), pp. 327–328.

[15]Charline Hill Brubaker, "What Are the Effects of a Two-Year Kindergarten Program on Academic Achievement in the Elementary Grades?" (unpublished Doctoral Dissertation, New York University, 1959).

[16]Elizabeth Mechem Fuller, *About the Kindergarten* (Washington, D.C.: American Educational Research Association, National Education Association, 1961), p. 13.

[17]Nila B. Smith, *Shall We Teach Formal Reading in the Kindergarten?* (Washington, D.C.: Association for Childhood Education International, 1964).

[18]Leonore Boehm, "Exploring Children's Thinking," *The Elementary School Journal*, No. 61 (April 1961), p. 371.

[19]Inhelder, *ibid.*, p. 372.

[20]Symposium, "Thinking," *Child Development*, No. 31, (1960), p. 239.

[21]Fuller, *op. cit.*, pp. 5–6.

[22]Ausubel, *op. cit.*, pp. 3–4.

[23]Willard C. Olson, *op. cit.*, p. 143.

[24]Helen Heffernan, "Pressures to Start Formal Instruction Early," *Don't Push Me!* (Washington, D.C.: Association for Childhood Education International), p. 18.

[25]Gertrude H. Hildreth, *Readiness for School Beginners* (New York: World Book Company, 1950).

[26]Ethyl Vandeburg, "Readiness for Language Arts Begins in the Kindergarten," *Elementary School Journal*, No. 53 (April 1953), pp. 448–452.

[27]Newell C. Kephart, *The Slow Learner in the Classroom* (Columbus, Ohio: Charles E. Merrill Books, Inc. 1960), p. 6.

[28]G. N. Getman and Elmer R. Kane, *The Physiology of Readiness* (Minneapolis: P.A.S.S., Inc., 1964), p. iii.

[29]Kephart, *op. cit.*, p. 63.

[30]*Ibid.*, pp. 61–63.

[31]*Ibid.*, p. 13.

[32]Benjamin S. Bloom, Allison Davis and Robert Hess, *Compensatory Education for Cultural Deprivation* (New York: Holt, Rinehart and Winston, Inc., 1966), p. 13.

[33]Kephart, *op. cit.*, p. 42.

[34]*Ibid.*, p. 44.

[35]*Ibid.*, p. 53.

[36]Eugene G. Roach and Newell C. Kephart, *Purdue Perceptual-Motor Survey* (Columbus, Ohio: Charles E. Merrill Books, Inc., 1966).

[37]Florence E. Sutphin, *Perceptual Testing-Training Handbook for First Grade Teachers* (Winter Haven, Florida: Boyd Brothers, Inc., 1964).

[38]Marianne Frostig and David Horne, *The Frostig Program for the Development of Visual Perception* (Chicago: Follett Publishing Company, 1964).

[39]Bloom, Davis and Hess, *op. cit.*, p. 45.

[40]Audrey Jackson, "The Administration of the Purdue Perceptual-Motor Survey to Disadvantaged Five-Year-Olds" (unpublished paper, Florida Atlantic University, July 1967).

[41]Katherine DiMeo, "Visual-Motor Skills: Response Characteristics and Pre-Reading Behavior" (unpublished Doctoral Dissertation, University of Miami, June 1967).

[42]David R. Miller and Guy E. Swanson, *Inner Conflict and Defense* (New York: Holt, Rinehart and Winston, 1960), quoted by Miriam Goldberg, "Factors Affecting Educational Attainment in Depressed Urban Areas," in A. Harry Passow (ed.), *Education in Depressed Areas* (New York: Columbia University Press, 1965), p. 94.

Chapter 10

Children of Poverty

Children of physical and spiritual poverty have always been with us. It is only recently, however, that they have been given the careful attention which all children warrant.

In the course of this "discovery" of the disadvantaged in our midst, we came to two fresh realizations. First, these youngsters are handicapped by their environments and have special problems. Second, we have not been meeting their needs within the public schools they are forced to attend as captive audiences. They are living proof that we demand compliance within highly structured, academically oriented environments which frequently have nothing to offer but sterile, meaningless material with little apparent relevance to the concerns of the learner. Teaching starts where the child is and goes on from there. Teaching involves fertile communication, vibrant interchange. To teach is to illuminate, to enlighten. We have not been teaching. The very fact that special programs have now been organized to take care of these children of physical and spiritual poverty such as the Baltimore Early Admissions, Head Start, and Migrant programs, Project Follow Through, Upward Bound, Higher Horizons—to name a few—is evidence that we have not been concerned enough about children as individuals to tailor programs to our admittedly diverse school population. These children whom we obviously have not reached are the living proof that what passes for teaching in the classrooms of our nation must be something far different.

The characteristics of the young child from a disadvantaged home environment which are most often noted are remarkably similar to those of any young child. For example, his interest in movement and action, contributing to a more physical style of learning, is common to all early childhood youngsters. His short attention span and difficulty with tasks requiring lengthy concentration and word-centered approaches are other familiar characteristics which can be generally discerned among young children. Here-and-now concerns contribute to a lack of interest in the future, the distant, the past. The early child-hood youngster, whether from an advantaged or disadvantaged back-ground, is most interested in the now, the present, the immediate. These characteristics are expressions of his developmental level. They are not peculiar to one segment of the population. All young chil-dren need enriched, stimulating environments. The foundation blocks building up to readiness and culminating in successful achieve-ment of formal academic skills in the later grades of the elementary school depend upon a wealth of meaningful seeing, hearing, express-ing, and doing on the part of all early childhood youngsters. And there is empirical evidence to support this broad program of activities based upon children's developmental levels, needs, and interests.

DEEP-SEATED PROBLEMS

It would seem, then, that programs designed with young children as individuals and as members of groups firmly in mind, should be able to stand as monuments of enlightenment. That they frequently do not may be attributed to two major causes. One of these causes has plagued classrooms at every level of the educational continuum: a teacher who is ill equipped to meet the demands of the job, either by temperament, training, competency, attitude, or all four. The second cause is actually intertwined with the first, but can also be considered separate: a basis misunderstanding of the life styles, culture, and spe-cial problems of the lower socioeconomic segments of the population.

> Teachers, middle-class themselves, find it rewarding to work with those whose values are like theirs. When they encounter the disadvantaged child, whose values and life style are different, they judge him in terms of their middle-class standards. Further, they often perceive him in terms of the absence of a culture, rather than the presence of a different set of standards and culture.[1]

The low socioeconomic level youngster who is truly disadvan-taged comes from a home background which is not nurturing him ade-quately. He brings to school with him his prior background experi-ences, as all children do. In his case, there may be severe deficits in all or some developmental areas. Bowlby indicated:

> It is noteworthy that conditions of extreme and prolonged sen-sory deprivation throughout the period of a chimpanzee's infancy

are found to result in permanent impairment accompanied by structural changes that can loosely be described as atrophy through disuse. Plainly much further research is required of which some must be on animals because it is unthinkable experimentally to subject human infants to the extreme and prolonged deprivation the effects of which it is necessary to investigate if some of these issues are to be settled. In the meantime, evidence is overwhelming that an organism—whether human or infra-human—develops through a process of constant interaction with its environment, and that to the extent that its environment is depriving its development will be retarded or distorted.[2]

These children of spiritual and physical poverty, then, exhibit symptoms of cognitive and affective deprivation. There may be a two year lag in language and concept development in comparison with youngsters of comparable age from nurturing home environments. They may be emotionally crippled, which in turn affects all other areas of growth. Physically, they are undernourished. They have had too little of what is needed for optimal growth and development and too much in the way of frustration, hard knocks, and failure. "I can't do it anyhow, so why try?" is expressive of their poor self-image. Zigler affirmed that, "Disadvantaged children are not motivated by what the middle class takes for granted. The lower-class child needs immediate and tangible reward. . . We are dealing with a child who expects to fail, who has no confidence. It is a reflection of his whole stance toward life."[3]

Where do we find the disadvantaged?

> The children commonly considered disadvantaged are the result of poverty; of chronically unemployed or unemployable fathers; of one-parent homes, frequently mother-dominated. They are city slum dwellers, rural uneducated farmhands, and migrants. They are children of unassimilated lowest social class Negroes, Puerto Ricans, American Indians, Mexican American, and Caucasians. They are one of every three city children who have too little of everything; too little living space, too little (and poor quality) food and sleep, too little personal attention, too little medical and nursing care when sick and too little correction of defects, too little energy and endurance, too little information about themselves and their world, too little curiosity (why ask when no one answers?), too little success, too little self-respect and self-confidence, too little reason to try, too little money and clothing, too little to play with and read, too little happiness.[4]

As Howe pointed out, deprived children come in assorted colors. Grambs reported on a study of the Negro:

The self that the Negro child learns early in life is one exposed to the most difficult of all situations for the human being to cope with; an inadequate family living on the edge of economic insufficiency. . . . .

The damage to the child's self esteem appears greater for Negro boys than for girls. Though it is debatable whether, in general, it is more or less difficult to grow up as a boy or as a girl in our culture, it seems clear from the evidence that during early childhood and school years, the Negro girl accommodates better to the circumstances of existence. . . . This can be accounted for in part by the fact that the male models available for the growing boy are themselves demoralized. . . . The fact that so many Negroes become contributing and stable members of society is an extraordinary tribute to the resilience of the human psyche.[5]

Bowlby, in discussing the effect of depriving experiences on development which have been emphasized in recent studies, stated:

Thus, the early findings of Spitz and Skeels, which once met with severe criticism, have been amply confirmed by subsequent studies; these have shown that deprivation causes retardation of development, that the retardation is progressive as deprivation is prolonged, and that language and social development are the specific processes most severely affected.[6]

He also underlines the urgency of determined action to reduce the number of deprived children in our midst, for they are the source of social infection as real and serious as any viral epidemic.[7]

Admittedly, these are deep-seated problems which require comprehension and wise intervention. Unfortunately, some of the attention being given to the efforts to provide compensatory programs for children in need of special help has been of the wait-and-see variety. It is a wait-and-see attitude which demands tangible achievements in formal academic subjects for satisfaction. After all, is the reasoning, these children have spent some time in school now; let them show what they can do.

Assessment

The special programs and projects which have attempted to aid the disadvantaged child seem to have been successful to a measurable degree in some cases. Other evidence suggests that there either has been no appreciable change, or if change is discernible at all, it is of short duration.

In summarizing reports in the literature on the effects of intervention programs on the intellectual functioning of preschool disadvantaged children, Hodges and Spicker stated that ". . . the intellectual functioning of disadvantaged children can be substantially raised by home intervention, preschool curriculum intervention, or a combination of both. No one approach, at this time, appears to be more effective than any other."[8] Brittain indicated: "Although preliminary findings concerning the effects of preschool enrichment programs are predominantly positive, this is not universally so. Gains in IQ scores and augmented language-cognitive ability have been found in several follow-up studies. . . . But this is not evenly true; some follow-up studies have not found such effects."[9] Why all this difficulty in measuring results? The data were often incomplete and the period in which the programs had been in operation was too short, hence it was not possible to draw absolute conclusions about the success or failure of these programs.[10]

Another one of the problems in studying the data is that the evidence of improvement within these disadvantaged young children is generally sought through scores on tests such as the Peabody Picture Vocabulary Test, The Illinois Test of Psycholinguistic Ability, The Columbia Mental Maturity Test, The Gates or Metropolitan Reading Readiness Tests, The Stanford-Binet Intelligence Scale, Philadelphia Verbal Abilities, Goodenough Draw-a-Man Test. It is difficult to measure changes in behavior and performance by means of paper-and-pencil approaches under the best of conditions. There is an ever-present danger, too, that programs will begin to reflect only the kinds of cognitive activities which can be directly measured as to results without regard for the highly sensitive and difficult to assess emotional-motivational areas. This would limit and restrict the school environments we provide to the point of arid sterility.

Need for Reevaluation

Zigler's and Butterfield's work throws doubt on the contention that the disadvantaged child's basic problem is an intellectual deficit. Our concern with the number of points the IQ score has been raised due to an enriched school environment and our use of this evidence as a sole criterion for the success or failure of an intervention program must be reevaluated. So-called changes in intellectual functioning may actually be changes in motivational functioning. The role of motivation in a child's measurable improvement has not, it seems, been adequately assessed.

The findings indicate that the deprived child suffers from an emotional and motivational deficit which decreases his usual intellectual performance to a lower level than we would expect from his intellectual potential as measured in an optimizing test situation. In trying to improve the deprived child's general level of performance, it would appear at least as important to attempt to correct his motivational inadequacies by developing nursery programs geared specifically toward changing his adverse motivational patterns as it is to concentrate on teaching cognitive skills and factual knowledge. . . . It would appear that such interventions should be assessed in terms of their success in fostering greater general competence among deprived children rather than their success in developing particular cognitive abilities alone.[11]

Longitudinal studies have highlighted the long-range effects which early deprivation of affection and gratification have upon children. These children are not free to extract what they need for further growth and development from even stimulating, enriched school environments, because they are still dependent, still searching for attention. Bowlby stressed that "mother-love in infancy and childhood is as important for mental health as are vitamins and proteins for physical health."[12] If the deficits in the affective domain are severe, then the child will spend his time in trying to fill his immediate, pressing needs for love and affection. This in turn will color his views of himself and others, as well as his motivation and general level of aspirations. The young child cannot be expected to evince genuine interest in deciphering the squiggles on a page in even the most fascinating book if he is convinced that he is unwanted, that no one really cares. The opening wedge with such a child is a patient, gradual build-up of trust in some consistent figure in his environment. By default, this figure often becomes the teacher. The patience, solicitude and understanding required are considerable.

It is important to understand the impulsive, hostile, aggressive behavior of some children, the sullen apathy and stubborn refusal to learn of others, and the self destructive, psychotic behavior of yet other children as conveying at least one kind of message: "I'm afraid of you. I'm afraid you'll treat me as I have been treated by other adults. I can only behave as I've learned to behave with others. I know no other way, until I'm shown that you are a different kind of person. But I'm afraid that you can't stick it out with me long enough for me to find out.". . .

We are . . . talking of "love" which is based on the desire to help another grow, develop, and live with himself and others with

greater satisfaction. Unfortunately for many children they need
to experience this kind of love before they can trust and respond to
affection and warmth as signs of encouragement and personal regard and concern.[13]

Solutions

In considering possible solutions to the problems of educating
our disadvantaged child populations, it has been proposed that special
classes composed of these disadvantaged within our school systems be
organized, starting with the early years and continuing throughout all
the levels of public education. This is recognition of a sort. However,
it is another futile attempt at homogeneous grouping with emphasis
placed upon the weaknesses of these youngsters and what must be
done to pull them up to some kind of acceptable level. There is no
recognition of the strengths which they could supply and we could utilize in our programs for all children. There is no admission of the fact
that a carefully designed program meets the needs of the separate individuals within it and is as strong as its concern for these individuals.
Nor is there awareness that heterogeneity in itself can provide many
resources for learning.

A deliberate infusion of these children into the middle socioeconomic level classrooms of our schools is necessary as well as smaller
classes in general. When students fill a classroom to the overflow
point, management deteriorates to a rigid holding of the line to avoid
skirmish. The size and ratio must be carefully worked out for optimal
results to occur, for if there are too many disadvantaged children in
proportion to advantaged within any group, the overall teaching-learn-
ing task becomes more difficult and the value of the group itself as
an educative vehicle will be diminished. Morsell, in disucssing the
conclusions of a study by Office of Education, indicated, "if a minority
pupil from a home without much educational strength is put with
school mates with strong educational backgrounds, his achievement is
likely to increase."[14]

Any significant solution must focus on attention to the needs of
the individual as a total entity. Programs based on the assumption that
all this young deprived child requires for academic success is a solid
background of academically oriented cognitive skills, a kind of New
England prep-school environment, are doomed to eventual failure.
Any program which emphasizes the neck-up child and fails to recognize the intertwined nature of all aspects of growth and develop-

ment is wasting valuable talent, potential, time, and money. Regard for the whole child is an indispensable yardstick in the determination of school environments for the disadvantaged.

In commenting on the successful results obtained from special pre-school projects for disadvantaged nursery and kindergarten youngsters in Racine, Baltimore, Nashville, New York, and Chicago, Spodek affirmed that each of the programs was rooted firmly "in the conventions of the nursery school and kindergarten."[15] He outlined, "The common areas of the curriculum stressed are the development of cognitive skills, language facility, self-concept, and motivational patterns, as well as an increase in environmental stimulation."[16] Deutsch emphasized, "Equally important, methods must be sufficiently flexible and play-oriented to be adaptable to the primary learning levels and personality organization characteristic of the infant and the young child."[17]

Osborn noted that the gains resulting from Head Start programs are encompassed in four areas; namely, a renewed interest in early childhood education as an important growth period, the development of the Child Development Center as both a concept and a community facility, improvement of the teacher-pupil ratio, and attitudinal changes which reflect mutual concerns and cooperation on the part of teachers and parents.[18]

Summary

The goals for the disadvantaged young child and for all early childhood youngsters must be long-range and have continuity throughout the levels of our educational enterprises. One-shot approaches are not only costly, they are self-defeating. As Tyler cautioned, "To develop a program that is highly effective requires the further education of personnel, the devising of curricula, teaching procedures and materials of instruction, and the testing and modification of plans and materials through evaluation experience."[19]

A clear picture emerges when the young, deprived child is offered a supportive, enriched, stimulating environment. Changes occur, some of which are noted by means of available measuring devices. For these children, the first and only contact with a child's garden, a utopian microcosm in which they count for something, takes place in an early childhood setting. Often, it is all too brief and abruptly ceases

Growth needs time out for wonder, for interest, for curiosity.

upon entrance to first grade. Hechinger warned that early compensatory education is of limited benefit unless there is follow-up. These children's preschool gains will erode unless they are constantly reinforced.[20]

There are discernible threads of quality woven into the educational tapestries designed for young disadvantaged children. The following pattern emerges:

1. Development of a positive self-image.
2. Development of feelings of trust in the teacher and other school personnel.
3. Growth of curiosity about the physical and social environment.
4. Development of receptive and expressive language skills—specifically vocabulary growth, verbal fluency, and spontaneity of expression.
5. Clarification and expansion of concepts.
6. Amplification of sensory and perceptual acuity.
7. Expansion of interest in books, stories, and the joys of reading.
8. Experiences with routines of school and in group living.

This is an effective pattern for children of poverty as well as for youngsters from middle and upper socioeconomic levels. It is a sound beginning for all young children.

NOTES

[1]Allan C. Ornstein, "Let's Start Reaching the Disadvantaged," *Kappa Delta Pi Record*, Vol. 4 (February 1968), p. 67.

[2]John Bowlby, *Child Care and the Growth of Love*. 2d ed. (Baltimore, Maryland. Penguin Books, 1966), p. 223.

[3]Edward Zigler, quoted in *National Conference on Education of the Disadvantaged* (United States Office of Education, July 1966), p. 10.

[4]Gertrude Noar, *Teaching the Disadvantaged What Research Says to the Teacher*, No. 33 (Washington, D.C.: Association of Classroom Teachers, a department of the National Education Association, 1967), pp. 3–4. By permission.

[5]Jean D. Grambs, "The Self-Concept: Basis for Re-education of Negro Youth," In Kvaraceus, etal, *Negro Self-Concept* (New York: McGraw-Hill Book Company, 1965), pp. 18, 20.

[6]Bowlby, *op. cit.*, p. 212.

[7]*Ibid.*, p. 239.

[8]Walter L. Hodges and Howard H. Spicker, "The Effects of Preschool Experiences on Culturally Deprived Children," *Young Children*, Vol. 23 (October 1967), p. 33.

[9]Clay V. Brittain, "Some Early Findings of Research on Preschool Programs for Culturally Deprived Children," *Children*, Vol. 13 (July–August 1966), in J. L. Frost (ed.), *Early Childhood Education Rediscovered* (New York: Holt, Rinehart and Winston, Inc., 1968), p. 287.

[10]*Racial Isolation in the Public Schools, Volume I* (Washington, D.C.: U.S. Government Printing Office, 1967), p. 127.

[11]Edward Zigler and Earl C. Butterfield, "Motivational Aspects of Changes in IQ Test Performance of Culturally Deprived Nursery School Children," *Child Development*, Vol. 39 (March 1968), p. 12. Reprinted by permission of the Society for Research in Child Development, Inc.

[12]Bowlby, *op. cit.*, p. 240.

[13]Irving N. Berlin, "Love and Mastery in Education," *The Educational Forum*, Vol. 31 (November 1966), pp. 47–48, by permission of Kappa Delta Pi, an Honor Society in Education.

[14]John A. Morsell, quoted in *National Conference on Education of the Disadvantaged, op. cit.*, p. 13.

[15]Bernard Spodek, "Poverty, Education and the Young Child," *Educational Leadership*, Vol. 22, May 1965, in *Teaching the Disadvantaged Young Child* (Washington, D.C.: National Association for Education of Young Children, 1966), p. 84.

[16]*Ibid.*, p. 84.

[17]Martin Deutsch, "Facilitating Development in the Pre-School Child: Social and Psychological Perspectives," *Merrill Palmer Quarterly of Behavior and Development*, Vol. 10 (July 1964), in Fred M. Hechinger (ed.), *Preschool Education Today* (New York: Doubleday and Company, Inc., 1966), p. 92.

[18]D. Keith Osborn, "Some Gains from the Head Start Experience," *Childhood Education*, Vol. 44 (September 1967), p. 8.

[19]Ralph W. Tyler, "The Task Ahead," *National Conference on Education of the Disadvantaged, op. cit.*, p. 63.

[20]Fred M. Hechinger, *Saturday Review*, December 18, 1965, p. 60.

Chapter 11

Kindergarten: A Step Up*

Childhood, that delightful period between emergence from the womb and the first furrows of adolescence, is under fire today. It is under fire by some of the very people who should be most aware of the importance of childhood itself as a period of indelible impressions: parents, educators, psychologists, scientists, sociologists, anthropologists, medical specialists.

Insidious pressures are being brought to bear upon children of all ages. The pressure to succeed is on, in a highly competitive race to a Mount Olympus emblazoned with middle-socioeconomic-oriented values. The pressure to succeed on an adult level and learn formal subject matter earlier than ever before has permeated even the kindergarten.

Achievements are important to man. They are the mark and measure of a civilization. But let us reexamine our thinking about the kindergarten-age child in our century. The only true measure of his growth is to compare him with himself, as he was before and as he is now. In our programs for this child we must be aware of his total development, with our world of today serving as a backdrop.

The time when a single man could encompass a dozen different fields of knowledge, as Aristotle did, is past. We do not ourselves know all that our children will need to know in the ever-expanding frontiers of the future. We do know that our children will have to be flexible. They will have to be good at thinking critically, boldly, creatively, imaginatively. They will need to be leaders as well as followers. They will have to be good at rolling with the punches in a world dramatically different from ours. We can help the kindergarten child to face this new world by considering his total development. This means not only his mind but his heart, body, emotions, and general adjustment to life and to the world as well.

As an important phase in the educational continuum, the kindergarten sets the stage for present success upon which later success can be built. This pays dividends for the child in the present and in the future.

How can these dividends be assured for the child who steps up into kindergarten? By planning with understanding. And the most effective planning starts with the realization that when a child goes to school he carries his head, his body and his heart with him. All of these need attention. Charles Calitri, in describing the disadvantaged child, comments:

> We have to understand that many of the children who sit in our classrooms are possessed of shattered dignity, frightened selves, and hostility too deep to be seen in their eyes. They have learned . . . that one can hide things from a people that has not yet discovered how to look at other people and know what they are seeing.[1]

Disadvantaged children are more vulnerable to failure due to lack of "school know-how," a paucity of educationally enriching experiences in their home environment, and a sense of personal inadequacy. As with all young children, it is important for the child of physical and spiritual poverty to establish and strengthen his own identity. A positive self-image is as necessary to his optimal growth and development as fresh air, food, and sunshine. The primary goal of educators, particularly in the early years of school, should be to help all children build a self-image of themselves as worthy, capable individuals. Full self-realization is not possible without this.

WHAT WE KNOW ABOUT LEARNING

The program in the kindergarten must reflect awareness of and sensitivity to a five-year-old's learning style. He learns as a child does, with a child's mind. It is the adult who can cope with a high level of abstract thinking dealing exclusively with verbal propositions, not he.

Research on learning has contributed to our understanding of how a young child forms concepts, how he can make learnings become a part of him.

We know that learning itself, an active dynamic process, is dependent upon a rich background of sensory and motor experiences. It has a better chance of proceeding in an environment which allows the child use of his five senses.

We know that bridges must be built to new learnings by connecting them to what the child already knows or has experienced. He needs learnings that are related, that fit together so that somehow he can see the connections. He can then build these related learnings into a structure. Integrating these learnings into a structure which means something to him and becomes a part of him takes place during a multisensory approach. It takes place while he manipulates objects in his environment, while he questions, solves problems, plays, and creates. It does not take place during a deskbound approach in which he is rooted to a chair with pencil, paper, and workbooks. He needs to practice what he learns by doing, by applying, by testing. The effective use of questions is an important technique. It primes and directs young minds to be curious, to explore, to reason, to solve problems creatively.

We know, then, that learning proceeds best under conditions which provide a wealth of diverse sensory-manipulative experiences. It proceeds best in an environment which primes the child to ask questions, to raise problems, to search for solutions, to discover and express himself in a variety of ways.

We also know that new interests and curiosities can be developed in a stimulating, satisfying, and attractive environment.

We know that he learns best by proceeding from concrete things to the abstract, from simple to complex things, from the immediate to the more remote. His mind develops as his words do—in the direction of the more complex. But this takes time. And some of us are in a hurry. We seem to be searching for formulas which will produce instant adults, an ever-present danger in this era of pushbutton results.

State of Being Ready to Proceed

A leisurely wait for signs of maturity and readiness is not the answer either. The good kindergarten program does not put a lid on the child. The lid is off. If he is ready for various learning experiences, these experiences will be provided, whether they are in the area of more formal reading and mathematics instruction, how to hold the pencil to keep it from slipping away, or how to cut with the scissors.

Readiness, or the state of being ready for something to proceed, is really quite simple to understand. It can be compared to the old saying, "You can lead a horse to water, but you can't make him drink." Let's paraphrase that: "You can lead a child to a book, but you can't make him read." It is important that the child not meet with frustration and failure in his beginning attempts to decipher those abstract symbols, words, and numbers. He can be helped to want to read by providing many firsthand experiences, by providing a wealth of direct contacts and vicarious experiences. He can be helped by providing him with time and opportunity to poke, probe, listen, watch, and do. In other words, he can be guided, encouraged, and stimulated by a breadth of experience and a broad program of purposeful activities to want to read—planned, of course, by a qualified teacher whose concern for each child is translated into understanding of his individual needs. Then, if the child's attitude is eager and if his green light is flashing the go-ahead signal, go-ahead it is!

There are some helpful, go-ahead signals. If a child displays most or all of these, his teacher will certainly provide him with opportunities to learn even more about that fascinating subject of reading.

- The child expresses his ideas well in speaking.
- He uses a large vocabulary and has good sentence structure.
- He can hear the different sounds in letters and in words.
- He can see differences in words and in letters.
- He has a wide variety of experiences to help make reading mean something to him. Experiences are the keys which unlock the meanings behind the words.
- He can remember well. This is important in reading. Drill in itself does not help his memory. Living widely and relating what happens now to what has gone before does help his memory.
- He is able to listen to and to follow directions.
- He is able to finish what he starts out to do. He has stick-to-itiveness.
- He can listen and attend to something in which he is interested for a length of time without becoming restless or fidgety.

The child is truly interested in finding out what those little squiggles on paper represent. He really wants to know all the time; he questions and wonders—not just once in a while but constantly. If he is not at this point now, there is no cause for worry. He will get there as surely as day follows night if he is healthy and normal. He will want to read in his own good time. Budding eagerness can be killed by parental or school pressures.

Health and Security at Home: A Child's Right

The child gets enough rest, good food, fresh air, and sunshine. This may seem obvious. It is. But it is important enough to bear repeating. A sick child cannot make the best effort of which he is capable. Nor can a tired child, or a weak child, or a hungry child.

The child feels secure at home. He feels his parents' affection, understanding, and love. He feels that he is liked as he is, for what he is. These are not withheld from him because he has not "measured up" somehow. This security is his right. It is as necessary for him as food, clothing, and shelter. An emotionally upset child cannot do his best. A child starved for love, attention, or recognition cannot learn anything well, much less reading.

Building upon Whole Learnings

The child enjoys listening to stories and looking at pictures. He loves to hear someone read to him and likes to pretend he is "reading" too.

He gets along well in a group of children. He does not need to be the center of attention in order to be happy and content. He can cooperate, work, and play with other children as well as by himself.

The child's score on readiness tests, culturally unbiased intelligence tests, and assessment inventories shows that he is ready for more formal instruction in reading. This score or scores should be just one indication among many, however. It would not be fair to pin a label on a child. It is fair to observe him in a wide variety of situations during his school day. And, of course, this observation should be carried on by an intelligent, professionally prepared, understanding, and sympathetic teacher.

The foundation blocks, then, building up to readiness and culminating in successful achievement of formal academic skills in the later grades of the elementary school, depend upon a special kind of program. It is a program which supplies and builds upon whole learnings. The child has difficulty with learnings that are arranged in bits and pieces, unrelated to one another. Unified experiences are most helpful, as well as subjects which arise naturally in the course of the school day.

Reading, as an example, is not one isolated period during the kindergarten day. It goes on all during the day: when a child needs scissors and walks to the box labeled *scissors*; when a child enjoys the colorful books on the library table; when teacher reads a story; when the children write a story, with the teacher's help, about a trip they all took; when the day's activities are discussed and teacher writes the morning's or afternoon's plans on the board; when a child speaks and listens to the sounds of another's words. Yes, reading and learning go on all during the kindergarten school day.

The child needs time and opportunity to develop in the whole area of language arts. Many opportunities are provided for listening and speaking. There is time and opportunity for reading informally the signs, lists, labels, captions, names, and charts in the room. If the child is truly ready for it, formal instruction in reading is carried on geared to his maturity and general readiness. A variety of methods are used, suited to the individual child's needs and his learning style. There is time to learn to write when this form of communication is needed and when the child is sufficiently mature.

Reading goes on all during the kindergarten program. Language arts does, too. And arithmetic, science, and social studies are woven into this meaningful tapestry. This is what is meant by "whole learnings."

Heart of Program: Concrete Experiences

Numbers are used by the child in a variety of ways. They are used in daily activities in real, problem-solving situations. To understand numbers, this child must have many concrete experiences in manipulating them, in using them in a variety of real or simulated situations. Then he will be able to move up from this base to more abstract levels in the later grades of the elementary school.

The social studies he learns are centered in home, family, school, and immediate neighborhood. At this stage in his development the young child is most interested in the here-and-now, in himself, in his family. Self-interest is very strong. Experiences he has in social studies center around interests and concerns in the world which he can see and which is expanding around him. His information-gathering is done directly because that is the way he learns best. He gathers this information from people, objects, the immediate community, trips, films, charts, pictures, and photographs. He begins to understand his cultural heritage by observing special holidays.

Science activities are geared to objects and phenomena which this youngster can see, observe, explore, and test by means of his five senses. He experiments with magnets, prisms, magnifying glasses, scales, plants, water, soil. He observes weather and weather instruments, temperature and seasonal changes, animals. He works with simple machines. Emphasis is on understanding the world around him and on methods of finding out why, what, how, and when. The basic method of science is observation, a firsthand look at nature. Firsthand experience, then, is at the heart of it.

It is at the heart of the entire early childhood program.

This kindergarten child learns best from concrete situations, rather than from the abstract which depends upon verbal explanation. Activities and experiences make impressions upon him. Observations which he makes and problems which he solves make impressions upon him.

Using Senses to Understand His World

Emphasis in this early childhood program, then, is on the child's understanding of the world around him and expanding of this world through his senses. He literally hears, sees, tastes, smells, and touches his way to understanding!

Good planning for the early childhood program recognizes these allies of learning: interest, curiosity, activity. The raw materials with which the program is fashioned are the activities and experiences, the interests and needs of the child. Also helping to fashion the program is his present stage of growth and development.

Learning is easier this way. It is not only easier. It is fun. The child's eagerness to learn more and more grows. His questions keep coming and keep growing. His explorations and experimentations take on new meaning as he looks for answers. He is ready for understanding.

THE BEST OF WHAT WE KNOW

Empirical evidence is available to support a program based upon activities in keeping with children's present levels of growth and development, needs, and interests. Children grow, build concepts, attitudes, and skills through interaction with their environment. This total environment at home and in school should reflect the best of what we know to be helpful for the young child, with an absence of harmful pressures and tensions.

This is the best kind of step up.

If the whole educational continuum reflected this enlightened concern and care for all children, plus understanding of their development and special childhood needs, our century would then begin to earn its title: "The Century of the Child."

NOTES

*Based upon an article in *Childhood Education* by E. L. Widmer by permission of the Association for Childhood Education International. Copyright 1967 by the Association for Childhood Education International.

[1]Charles J. Calitri, "Language and Dignity of Youth," *Saturday Review*, July 20, 1963, p. 61.

Suggested Readings

American Educational Research Association, NEA. *School Plant and Equipment.* Washington, D.C.: The Association, 1951.

Anderson, Verna D., et al. *Readings in the Language Arts.* New York: The Macmillan Company, 1964.

Antin, Clara. *Blocks in the Curriculum.* New York: Early Childhood Education Council.

Applegate, Mauree. *Easy in English.* New York: Harper & Row, Publishers, 1960.

Ashton-Warner, Sylvia. *Teacher.* New York: Simon and Schuster, 1963.

Association for Childhood Education International. *Equipment and Supplies, No. 39.* Washington, D.C.: The Association, 1964.

———. *Portfolio for Kindergarten Teachers, 1960. Nursery School Portfolio-1961.* Washington, D.C.: The Association.

———. *Space, Arrangement, Beauty in School.* Washington, D.C.: The Association, 1958.

Aurback, H. A. *Selected Bibliography on Socioculturally Disadvantaged Children and Youth.* Pittsburgh: Learning Research and Development Center, 1966.

Bailey, Matilda, et al. *Language Learnings-Kindergarten, Grade 1, Grade 2.* New York: American Book Company, 1956.

Beck, John M., and Richard W. Safe. *Teaching the Culturally Disadvantaged Pupil.* Springfield, Ill.: Charles C. Thomas, 1965.

Bell, N. W., and E. F. Vogel (eds.). *A Modern Introduction to the Family.* New York: Free Press, 1960.

Bereiter, Carl S., and S. Engleman. *Teaching Disadvantaged Children in the Preschool.* Englewood Cliffs, N.J.: Prentice-Hall, Inc., 1966.

Beyer, Evelyn, and Jessie Stanton. *First Hand Experiences and Sensory Learning*. New York: Bank Street College Publication.

Bloom, Benjamin S., Allison Davis, and Robert Hess. *Compensatory Education for Cultural Deprivation*. New York: Holt, Rinehart and Winston, Inc., 1965.

Blough, Glenn O., and A. J. Huggett. *Elementary School Science and How to Teach It*. 4th ed. New York: Holt, Rinehart, and Winston, Inc., 1969.

Bond, Guy L., and Eva Bond Wagner. *Teaching the Child to Read*. 3rd ed. New York: The Macmillan Company, 1960.

Burns, Paul C., and Alberta Lowe. *The Language Arts in Childhood Education*. Chicago: Rand McNally, 1966.

Carrillo, Lawrence W. *Informal Reading Readiness Experiences*. California: Chandler Publishing Company, 1964.

Cheyney, Arnold B. *Teaching Culturally Disadvantaged in the Elementary School*. Columbus, Ohio: Charles E. Merrill Books, 1967.

Clark, Kenneth. *Prejudice and Your Child*. 2d ed. Boston: Beacon Press, 1963.

Cowles, Milly (ed.). *Perspectives in the Education of Disadvantaged Children*. New York: World Book Company, 1967.

Crosby, M. (ed.). *Language Programs for the Disadvantaged*. The Report of the NCTE Task Force on Teaching English to the Disadvantaged. Champaign, Ill.: National Council of Teachers of English, 1965.

————. *An Adventure in Human Relations*. New York: Follett Publishing Company, 1965.

Crow, Lester D., Walter I. Murray, and Hugh H. Smythe. *Educating the Culturally Disadvantaged Child*. New York: David McKay Company, Inc., 1966.

D'Amico, Victor E. *Creative Teaching in Art*. Scranton, Pa.: International Textbook Company, 1953.

Davis, A. *Social-Class Influences Upon Learning*. Cambridge: Harvard University Press, 1948.

Educational Research Council of Greater Cleveland. *Key Topics in Mathematics for the Primary Teacher*. Chicago: Science Research Associates, 1962.

Englehardt, N. L., N. L. Englehardt, Jr., and Leggett Stanton. *School Planning and Building Handbook*. New York: E. W. Dodge Corporation, 1956.

Franklin, Adele. *Blocks, A Tool of Learning.* New York: Bank Street College Publication.

————. *Home Play and Play Equipment.* Washington, D.C.: Children's Bureau.

Freeman, Kenneth, et al. *Helping Children Understand Science.* New York: John G. Winston Company, 1954.

Frost, J. L. (ed.). *Early Childhood Education Rediscovered: Readings.* New York: Holt, Rinehart and Winston, Inc., 1968.

————, and G. R. Hawkes. *The Disadvantaged Child: Issues and Innovations.* Boston: Houghton Mifflin Company, 1966.

Frostig, Marianne, and David Horne. *The Frostig Program for the Development of Visual Perception.* Chicago: Follett Publishing Company, 1964.

Gaitskell, Charles, and Margaret Gaitskell. *Art Education in the Kindergarten.* 3rd ed. Peoria, Ill.: Charles A. Bennett Company, Inc., 1962.

Gans, Roma. *Common Sense in Teaching Reading.* Indianapolis, Indiana: Bobbs-Merrill Company, 1963.

Getman, G. N., and Elmer R. Kane. *The Physiology of Readiness.* Minneapolis, Minnesota: P. A. S. S., Inc., 1964.

Gnagey, William J. *Controlling Classroom Misbehavior.* Washington, D.C.: National Education Association, 1965.

Goodman, Mary Ellen. *Race Awareness in Young Children.* New York: Collier Books, 1964.

Gordon, I. J., et al. *An Inter-Disciplinary Approach to Improving the Development of Culturally Disadvantaged Children.* Gainesville, Florida: University of Florida Press, 1966.

Gordon, E. W. *Compensatory Education for Disadvantaged Programs and Practices: Preschool through College.* New York: Yeshiva University, 1966.

Gray, Susan W., et al. *Before First Grade: The Early Training Project for Culturally Disadvantaged Children.* New York: Columbia University Press, 1966.

Harrington, M. *The Other America: Poverty in the United States.* New York: The Macmillan Company, 1962.

Hochman, Vivienne. *Trips in Early Childhood Education.* New York: Bank Street College Publication, 1967.

Hodges, W. L., et al. *The Development of a Diagnostically Based Curriculum for Psycho-Socially Deprived Preschool Children.*

Bloomington, Indiana: Institute for Child Study, Indiana University, 1965.

Holt, John, *How Children Learn.* New York: Pitman Publishing Corp., 1967.

────── . *The Underachieving School.* New York: Pitman Publishing Corporation, 1969.

Hymes, James L. Jr. *Before the Child Reads.* New York: Harper & Row, Publishers, 1958.

────── . *Behavior and Misbehavior.* Englewood Cliffs, N.J.: Prentice-Hall, Inc., 1955.

Ilg, Frances, and Louis Ames. *School Readiness.* New York: Harper and Row, publishers, 1964.

Jacobson, Willard S., and Harold Tannenbaum. *Modern Elementary School Science.* New York: Teachers College Bureau of Publications, 1961.

Keliher, Alice V. *Talks With Teachers.* Darien, Connecticut: Educational Publishing Corporation, 1958.

Kellogg, Rhoda, and Scott O'Dell. *The Psychology of Children's Art.* New York: Random House, Inc., 1967.

Kephart, Newell Carlyle. *The Slow Learner in the Classroom.* Columbus, Ohio: Charles E. Merrill Books, 1962.

Knight, M., et al. *Activities for the Early Development of Perceptual Skills.* University City, Missouri: University City School District, 1966.

Kohl, Herbert R. *Teaching the Unteachable.* New York: New York Review Books, 1967.

Kvaraceus, W. C. (ed.). *Negro Self-Concept: Implications for School and Citizenship.* New York: McGraw-Hill Book Company, 1965.

Leavitt, Jerome E. *The True Book on Tools for Building.* Chicago: Children's Press, Inc., 1955.

Lewis, M. M. *Language, Thought and Personality.* New York: Basic Books, Inc., 1963.

Lowenfeld, Viktor. *Your Child and His Art.* New York: The Macmillan Company, 1965.

Lucas & Newfeld. *Developing Pre-Number Ideas.* New York: Holt, Rinehart and Winston, Inc., 1965.

Mackintosh, Helen K., Lillian Gore, and Gertrude M. Lewis. *Educating Disadvantaged Children Under Six.* Washington, D.C.: Office of Education, U.S. Government Printing Office, 1965.

Mearnes, Hughes. *Creative Power: The Education of Youth in the Creative Arts.* 2d ed. New York: Dover Publications, Inc., 1958.

Moffitt, Mary W. *Woodworking for Children.* New York: Early Childhood Education Council.

Mueller, Francis J. *Modern School Math, Its Structure & Concepts.* Englewood Cliffs, N.J.: Prentice-Hall, Inc., 1965.

Murray, Ruth Lovell. *Dance in the Elementary School.* New York: Harper and Row, Publishers, 1963.

Murray, Thomas R. *Social Differences in the Classroom: Social Class, Ethnic and Religious Problems.* New York: David McKay Company, Inc., 1965.

National Association for the Education of Young Children. *Teaching the Disadvantaged Young Child.* Washington, D.C.: The Association, 1966.

———. *Let's Play Outdoors.* New York: The Association, 1966.

———. *Water, Sand and Mud as Play Materials.* New York: The Association, 1959.

———. *Space for Play.* Washington, D.C.: The Association, 1966.

Navarra, John G. *Science Today for the Elementary School Teacher.* New York: Harper & Row, Publishers, 1960.

———. *The Development of Scientific Concepts in a Young Child.* New York: Columbia University Press, 1955.

National Education Association. Department of Elementary-Kindergarten-Nursery Education. *Prevention of Failure.* Washington, D.C.: The Association, 1965.

New Jersey State Department of Education. The Compass. *Reading in the Kindergarten?* Trenton, N.J.: The Department, 1962.

———. The Compass. *Shall We Teach Formal Reading in Kindergarten?* Trenton, N.J.: The Department, 1964.

New York State Education Department. *Basic Considerations for the Kindergarten Program.* Albany, New York: The Department, 1959.

———. *Equipment for Children in Kindergarten.* Albany, New York: The Department, 1960.

———. *Guides for Selection of Indoor and Outdoor Equipment and Materials.* Albany, New York: The Department, 1966.

Miel, Alice, and Peggy Brogan. *More Than Social Studies.* Englewood Cliffs, N.J.: Prentice-Hall, Inc., 1957.

Niemeyer, J. *Programs for the Educationally Disadvantaged.* Washington, D.C.: U.S. Office of Education Bulletin, No. 17 (OE-34044), 1963.

Office of Education. *A Chance for a Change: New School Programs for the Disadvantaged*. Washington, D.C.: U.S. Office of Education, 1966.

Passow, A. Harry (ed.). *Education in Depressed Areas*. New York: Columbia University Press, 1963.

Perception Development Research Associates. *A Motor Perceptual Development Handbook of Activities*. La Porte, Texas: Perception Development Research Associates, 1966.

Potts, A. M. *Knowing and Educating the Disadvantaged, An Annotated Bibliography*. Alamosa, Colorado: The Center for Cultural Studies, 1964.

Reissman, Frank. *The Culturally Deprived Child*. New York: Harper and Row, Publishers, 1962.

Roach, Eugene G., and Newell C. Kephart. *Purdue Perceptual-Motor Survey*. Columbus, Ohio: Charles E. Merrill Books, Inc., 1966.

Robison, Helen F., and Bernard Spodek. *New Directions in the Kindergarten*. New York: Columbia University Press, 1965.

Scott, Louise B., and J. J. Thompson. *Talking Time*. New York: McGraw-Hill Book Company, 1966.

Shane, Harold G., et al. *Beginning Language Arts Instruction With Children*. Columbus, Ohio: Charles E. Merrill Company, 1961.

Sheckles, Mary. *Building Children's Science Concepts*. New York: Columbia University Press, 1958.

Sheehy, Emma. *There's Music in Children*. New York: Holt, Rinehart and Winston, Inc., 1952.

———. *Children Discover Music and Dance, A Guide for Parents and Teachers*. New York: Holt, Rinehart and Winston, Inc., 1959.

Siks, Geraldine Brain. *Creative Dramatics, An Art for Children*. New York: Harper and Brothers, 1958.

Smith, James A. *Creative Teaching of the Language Arts*. Boston: Allyn and Bacon, Inc., 1967.

Sonquist, H. D., and C. K. Kamii. *The Application of Some Piagetian Concepts to Teaching in a Preschool for Disadvantaged Children*. Ypsilanti, Michigan: Ypsilanti Public Schools, 1966.

Spodek, B. *Poverty, Education and the Young Child*. Washington, D. C.: National Association for Education of Young Children, 1965.

Starks, Esther B. *Blockbuilding*. Washington, D.C.: National Education Association.

Stern, C., and T. Gould. *Children Discover Reading*. New York: Random House, Inc., 1965.

Sutton, Elizabeth, *Knowing and Teaching the Migrant Child.* Washington, D.C.: Department of Rural Education of the National Education Association, 1962.

Taba, Hilda, and Deborah Elkins. *Teaching Strategies for the Culturally Disadvantaged.* Chicago: Rand, McNally and Company, 1966.

Tannenbaum, Harold E., and Nathan Stillman. *Science Education for Elementary School Teachers.* Boston: Allyn and Bacon, Inc., 1960.

Taylor, Jeanne. *Child's Book of Carpentry.* New York: Greenberg Publishers, 1948.

Taylor, K. W. *Teaching the Disadvantaged Young Child.* Washington, D.C.: National Association for Education of Young Children, 1966.

Usdan, Michael D., and Frederick Bertolaet (eds.). *Teachers for the Disadvantaged.* Chicago: Follett Publishing Company, 1966.

Van Dyke, Phyllis. *Trails in Kindergarten: How to Use Handicrafts in Preparing Children for Grade School.* New York: Exposition Press, 1959.

Webster, Staten (ed.). *Knowing the Disadvantaged.* San Francisco: Chandler Publishing Company, 1966.

Weikert, D. P. *Results of Preschool Intervention Programs.* Ypsilanti, Michigan: Ypsilanti Public Schools, 1966.

Weinberg, Meyer (ed.). *Learning Together, A Book on Integrated Education.* Chicago: Integrated Education Associates, 1964.

Zim, Herbert S. *Science for Children and Teachers.* Washington, D.C.: Association for Childhood Education International, 1953.

Index

177